AHEAD OF
HIS TIME:

WILHELM
PFEFFER

EARLY
ADVANCES IN
PLANT
BIOLOGY

AHEAD OF HIS TIME:

WILHELM PFEFFER

EARLY ADVANCES IN PLANT BIOLOGY

BY

ERWIN BÜNNING

TRANSLATED BY
HELMUT WILLIAM PFEFFER

Carleton University Press
Ottawa, Canada
1989

©Carleton University Press Inc. 1989

ISBN 0-88629-102-X (paperback)
    0-88629-103-8 (casebound)

Printed and bound in Canada

Carleton Science Series #1

Canadian Cataloguing in Publication Data
Bünning, Erwin, 1906-
    Ahead of his time

    Translation of: Wilhelm Pfeffer : Apotheker,
    Chemiker, Botaniker, Physiologe, 1845-1920.
    ISBN 0-88629-103-8 (bound) —
    ISBN 0-88629-102-X (pbk.)

    1. Pfeffer, Wilhelm Friedrich Philipp, 1845-1920.
    2. Botanists—Germany—Biography.   I. Title.

    QK31.P45B8313 1989   581'.092'4   C89-090353-0

Distributed by: Oxford University Press Canada,
                70 Wynford Drive,
                Don Mills, Ontario,
                Canada. M3C 1J9
                (416) 44-2941

Cover Design: Robert Chitty

Acknowledgements

Carleton University Press gratefully acknowledges the support
extended to its publishing programme by the Canada Council and the
Ontario Arts Council.

────────────

This translation is from the original German edition, Wilhelm Pfeffer:
Apotheker, Chemiker, Botaniker, Physiologe 1845-1920, © 1975
Wissenschaftliche Verlagsgesellschaft, MbH, Stuttgart, Federal
Republic of Germany. All rights reserved.

Contents

vi

vii

TRANSLATOR'S NOTE

It is my hope that this translation of Professor Erwin Bünning's book will allow English-speaking readers to become acquainted with the life and works of Wilhelm Pfeffer, a pioneer of modern experimental botany and biology. I have tried to make the translation clear and fluent, but I have taken care to preserve scientific accuracy. Professor Bünning agreed that I should translate freely, provided the essence of his account remained.

In 1899, Professor Alfred Ewart in his translation of Volume I of Pfeffer's *Physiology of Plants* wrote, "the difficulty of the original German has necessitated the exercise of a certain freedom in the process of translation . . ." For the same reason, I have broken down some of Pfeffer's involved, long sentences into shorter ones; however, I was careful to include all the points of the original statements.

I am very indebted to Dr. Martin Canny, Biology Department, Carleton University for his invaluable help in checking the terminology and the scientific statements of the translation. He also kindly prepared the photographic reproductions of the figures in the book. For this, and for his help in interesting Carleton University Press to publish the book, my special thanks. I wish to thank Professor Julius Adler, Department of Biochemistry, University of Wisconsin — Madison, for persuading me to undertake the translation. I also owe thanks to the following for their contributions: Professor Margaret McCully, Biology Department, Carleton University; Mrs. Marga Wohl of Madison, Wisconsin; Mr. Edward DeWath of San Francisco, California; and my wife Gladys.

FOREWORD

It was with pleasure that I followed the suggestion of Dr. Heinz Degen to write about the life and work of Wilhelm Pfeffer for the series "Grosse Naturforscher." This was not done to rescue Pfeffer from oblivion; he has not been forgotten. In fact, he has been quoted more frequently in recent times than in the first decades after his death. This occurred not in reference to minor questions of plant physiology, but rather in reference to major questions of general biology.

After my second reading of Pfeffer's works — some forty to fifty years after my first reading — I realized that they were already programmed into modern biology to a greater extent than I had originally perceived, and also to a greater extent than younger biologists who have not read Pfeffer's *Handbuch* could imagine.

I have tried to write in such a manner that non-biologists may also be able to appreciate Pfeffer's achievements. For this purpose, I have added some illustrations which physiologists may disregard. Other illustrations (figs. 11 and 16) should be of value in recalling results that were achieved at the start of this century.

I owe thanks to many who have helped me. First, I wish to mention Dr. H. William Pfeffer of Ottawa, Canada, grandson of Wilhelm Pfeffer. He sent me many family records and copies of letters, along with written and taped information on family recollections. I also thank Mr. Hermann Augustin, owner of the pharmacy in Grebenstein where Pfeffer was born, for providing Dr. Pfeffer's address and for sending me photographs of the pharmacy. Professor Hermann Ulrich, former director of the Institute of Agricultural Botany of the University of Bonn, supplied much information, as well as copies of records and photographs, one of which was used for figure 19. His personal recollections were an important contribution for chapter 18. For copies of letters and other documents, I owe thanks to the archives of the University of Tübingen (Dr. Schäfer), to the Archives of the State of Hesse, and to Dr. Horstmann. The portrait of Pfeffer (frontispiece) and the photograph of the Botanical Institute in Leipzig were provided through the kind efforts of the Leopoldina Archives in Halle (Professor Uschmann). Information from Japan was obtained from Dr. Tazawa (Osaka) and Professor Takahashi (Kurashiki).

Mrs. Brigitte Rätze took care of all the correspondence and of the manuscript. To her, many thanks.

Tübingen, Spring 1975   Erwin Bünning

1

INTRODUCTION AND
SOME IMPORTANT DATES
IN PFEFFER'S LIFE

Wilhelm Pfeffer is known as a botanist; he was an *Ordinarius* [full professor] of Botany at universities in Basel, in Tübingen, and in Leipzig. This would not have come about, had it not been for the support of farsighted men who knew how to evaluate Pfeffer's talent. He had not obtained the Arbitur certificate [matriculation from high school]. In spite of this fact, he was admitted to university. Even then, it would have seemed more appropriate for him to have become a pharmacist or a chemist, certainly not a botanist. By training he was a pharmacist. After four semesters of study and a thesis in chemistry, he graduated with a doctorate at the age of twenty-one. It was only afterwards that he turned more intensively to botany.

No one has surpassed Pfeffer's achievements in plant physiology, either in scope or in value. The importance of his achievements has been acknowledged in the field of physical chemistry and in the development of van't Hoff's Theory of Solutions. It should not be forgotten that Pfeffer pointed out the major problems which would face general biology in the twentieth century, and that he also proposed how these problems should be tackled. Pfeffer's achievements were honoured on the occasion of his seventieth birthday[1] and later in obituaries;[2] however, in the light of the latest advances in biology, his achievements now appear much more significant than his contemporaries could ever have imagined.

There were few botanists at the time who comprehended Pfeffer's objectives and the programs he proposed for use in general physiology. For this reason, I shall try to show how Pfeffer's ideas and the course he followed lead into present-day biology.

Important Dates in Pfeffer's Life

Wilhelm Friedrich Phillip Pfeffer

1845	Born March 9, in Grebenstein, [Hessia]
1860	End of school, start of apprenticeship
1863	Passed examination as apothecary's assistant
1865	Graduated with a Dr. Phil. from the University of Göttingen. Title of thesis in Chemistry: *Some Derivatives of Glycerin and Their Conversion into Allyls*
1868	Passed government examination in pharmacy in Marburg
1869-1870	Private assistant to Nathanael Pringsheim in Berlin
1870-1871	Worked with Julius Sachs in Würzburg
1871	*Habilitation* [appointment to the faculty] at the University of Marburg. Habilitation thesis: *The Effect of Coloured Light on the Decomposition of Carbon Dioxide in Plants*

1873	Assistant Professor at the University of Bonn
1877	Professor at the University of Basel
1878	Professor at the University of Tübingen
1884	Marriage to Henriette Volk
1887	Professor at the University of Leipzig
1894	Honorary Dr. med., University of Halle Honorary Dr. med., University of Königsberg
1906	Honorary Sc.D., Cambridge University
1911	Honorary Dr., University of Christiania (now Oslo)
1920	January 30, gave his last lecture January 31, death February 5, cremation in Leipzig

Pfeffer's move from Basel to Tübingen was reasonable. Tübingen had the better botanical institute, and it is here that the famous botanists von Mohl and Hofmeister had worked with great success. However, the move from Tübingen to Leipzig may seem puzzling. Many years later, W. Ruhland wrote that, "the . . . years spent in the pleasant Swabian town of the Muses on the River Neckar may well have been the happiest years in Pfeffer's life."[2] In fact, before he moved to Leipzig, Pfeffer wrote in his letters that he often felt homesick for the institute and for the beautiful surroundings in Tübingen. What he did not like was the "quality of the town."[3] Unlike von Mohl, he was not a bachelor, and he was not a Swabian.

The "quality" of Tübingen at the time is probably best illustrated by the following anecdote from a book on von Mohl by R. Braun-Artaria:

> Hugo von Mohl . . . would never have accepted a call away from Tübingen, he was totally attached to the town, its manners and its customs. One

3

evening von Mohl was sipping his beer at a crowded table at the "Post", when a young Prussian, recently appointed to the university, spoke disparagingly of the poor manners of a colleague. The young man concluded, "the fellow doesn't even own gloves!" "Sir!" shouted the old von Mohl, "do you think anyone here owns gloves?" Embarrassed, the young man stuttered, "but — you must". "Gloves" . . . von Mohl roared with laughter as he stretched his brown paw-like hands across the table, much to the merriment of the crowd.

In Pfeffer's time, Tübingen may still have presented itself the way Goethe wrote about it in 1797: "With all the manure, the streets are terribly dirty."[4]

Von Mohl was one of Pfeffer's predecessors at the university, during the years 1835 to 1872. Von Mohl was a bachelor, while Pfeffer was married by the time he decided to leave Tübingen. In making this decision, Pfeffer may have been influenced by his wife who was very conscious of her social standing, and who put much value on correct manners. Her grandson remembers that when he was a boy and visited with her in Leipzig, she would always insist on formal table manners during meals.

2
BASIC PERCEPTION OF
NATURAL SCIENCE

a) A Life Devoted to Science

"The human mind is as incapable of comprehending the ultimate meaning of things as it is incapable of comprehending infinity. Newton was absolutely right when he said that he who looks for the ultimate meaning of things, thereby reveals that he is not a man of science" (Pfeffer, 1904, p.4).

Pfeffer was indeed a man of science. One might be tempted to say that he was a man who was interested only in natural science; yet, he did not minimize the importance of other fields. There have been many great scientists who turned to fine arts in their leisure hours, and there have been some who asked questions about "the ultimate meaning of things," perhaps because they wished to show that the answer could not be found in scientific work. To balance his interest in the sciences, Pfeffer cultivated human relationships and a love of the outdoors. He particularly loved the high mountains. As a young man, he was the fifth person to climb the Matterhorn; and in his later years, he spent most of his vacations in the mountains. However, central to his life was his research and his teaching — it was biology, physics and chemistry from early morning to late at night.

Still, he was interested in events around him. "He was not the caricature of the German professor who remains disinterested in major events of the day. He kept abreast of current issues, including political matters and the happenings affecting the fatherland. Here, as always, he showed moderation in presenting his opinion."[5]

There were few outside events in Pfeffer's life. The routine of his research work and his teaching was occasionally interrupted by the vacations in the mountains, and by the receptions in Germany and abroad where he was given decorations and awards. Pfeffer appreciated these awards, and for his wife, these receptions were social highlights.

The events surrounding his death seem to be in accord with his style of life. On January 30, 1920, Pfeffer gave his last lecture in physiology, speaking with vigour and great mental alertness. After the lecture, he returned home and told his wife, "How blessed it would have been if I could have dropped dead right there." His colleague, H. Fitting, tells us, "there again followed lonely hours of deep brooding, deep depression . . . . In the evening of January 31st at 7 o'clock, the long desired end came without pain."[2a]

To a large extent, Pfeffer's success was built on his basic perception of science. He completely disapproved of the explanation that a vital force played a role in nature — a concept that has been promoted over and over again after his time.

b) All Processes of Life Have a Physical Explanation

In 1892, Pfeffer wrote:

> The conversion and utilization of energy in the growth of an organism may appear to be ever so intricate; however, this involves only the transforma-

tion and utilization of energy that reaches the organism from the outside. Thus, the same energy could have acted on dead matter in some other place just as readily. This consideration and the principle of the conservation of energy (which like the conservation of matter is basic to all natural sciences) exclude the existence of a specific form of energy (force) which supports life. The above merely expresses the consequence of the principle of causality, a requirement recognized in any sound teaching of physiology. This applies no matter how incomplete today's insights may be, and it applies even though it is questionable whether the full causal explanation of life's mechanism will ever be achieved (1892a, p.254).

However, if our inability to understand life's mechanism is to be construed as a sufficient reason to advocate a vital force in life, then we have to allow the Australian aborigine the right to attribute a special incomprehensible force to a music box or a clock — items which are totally outside of his experience (1897, p.5).

It is rather sad that decades later, Hans Driesch who started as a successful experimental zoologist, still acted like the Australian aborigine of Pfeffer's story. (The comparison could only be thought of as a slur by the person who underestimates the difficult position faced by a man of the Stone Age.) According to Driesch, the proof for the doctrine of vitalism went something like this: it is inconceivable that a machine which operates in three directions could at will divide, multiply or regenerate itself. However, a few decades later, this very machine was being analysed by molecular biologists. After Watson and Crick discovered the double helix of the genetically determining deoxyribonucleic acid, we have a fairly good idea of how this machine performs all the feats which Driesch considered to be "unthinkable." As an aside (I apologize for the gloss), the Papuas of New Guinea made use of the very same reasoning which Pfeffer conceded to the Australian aborigine[6] — another one of Pfeffer's "prophesies" (cf. p. 40).

In the cases where the known laws of physics and chemistry could not explain physiological processes, Pfeffer, contrary to others, did not assume the existence of a special vital force; instead, he demanded a more careful examination of these laws. His *Osmotische Untersuchungen* [*Osmotic Investigations*] may serve as an appropriate example. The opening statement of the book (cf. p. 29) represents the essence of scientific research, in no less a manner than the investigations which led to the discovery of the planet Neptune.

The existence of Neptune was initially postulated by applying Newton's laws — in the conviction of their universal validity — to the apparently inexplicable deviation in the course of the planet Uranus. Notwithstanding the doubters, Neptune was eventually identified in the calculated position. Pfeffer owes his discoveries to convictions of a similar kind. As a parallel to the manner in which Neptune was discovered, Pfeffer's plasma membrane of molecular dimensions was found to exist "in the calculated position" only after the electron microscope was invented. Until then, the existence of this plasma membrane was vigorously questioned for five decades.[7]

c) The Complexity of Life's Processes Is Often Overlooked

Pfeffer was not one to draw conclusions carelessly from chemistry and physics; he was fully aware of the complexities of biological processes. In his day, especially in the second half of the nineteenth century, it was not uncommon to have biological phenomena explained in simple physical terms. To a degree, this was a kind of "over-compensation" after vitalistic and speculative reflections on nature had been widely rejected. Pfeffer strongly repudiated simplifications which did not do justice to the complexity of biological processes: "In fact, similar results are frequently obtained by various methods, but an exterior similarity ... does not allow us to draw the conclusion that the interior causes are the same." As an example, he stressed that the division of protoplasts could not be simply the consequence of physical surface tension, as some other workers were suggesting. He also rejected the attempt to explain the arrangement of walls and lamellae in plant tissue as being comparable to the structure of a soap lather. In these cases, and in many other cases, he recognized a much greater degree of complexity than did Julius Sachs and other biologists. At the time, Jacques Loeb obtained excellent results in experiments to stimulate development without fertilization, and with experiments in regeneration. This led Loeb to become overly optimistic, and there were other researchers who felt the same way. It was believed that the action of simple physical forces was the cause of many physiological processes, such as in the case of the movement of amoeba. Pfeffer doubted these conclusions, and gave his reasons why (1904):

> All natural sciences converge towards a common ground in the fundamentals and in their final aims. Furthermore, if one considers that the division into separate disciplines is only a creation of human perception and abstraction, then it seems useless to argue whether physiology, or even astronomy are coordinate or subordinate to physics and chemistry. In the same sense, each of these disciplines can lay claim to independence. Physiology, in particular, has

as its final goal the task to investigate the significance and the use of the elemental substances and forces available in the universe for the building and functioning of living organisms. This may well be the most difficult and most complex problem facing us on our planet. It is obvious that a successful insight into the wondrous mechanism of a living organism is only possible with an intensive study of simple relationships, and with an energetic support from chemistry and physics.

Just as physics and chemistry of an earlier century had no inkling of the telephone or of aniline dyes and of their various applications, so we can state with certainty that the present range of experience in physics, chemistry and other sciences does not permit us to examine and to understand the totality of all combinations, constellations, and applications of the forces and substances which serve the organism. Similarly, it would be just as difficult for a person who has barely learned to read, to then foresee and understand the wealth of information which can be conveyed by means of an infinite combination of letters and words (1897, p.5-6).

Pfeffer expressly demanded that physiological processes should be traced back in a logical manner to the basic laws of physics and chemistry:

In all areas of scientific research, the striving for final goals eventually leads one to complex properties (the entity of scholastic philosophy) which we cannot break down, or do not wish to break down any further. Examples of such properties are cohesion, elasticity, and gravity. Some day, we may succeed to further dissect the atoms and the manifold properties associated with them. In principle, physiology stands on the same foundation as other natural sciences, even though it has to accept, as a given, complex properties or functions which cannot be further subdivided at present. In physiology, we are not able to relate the processes of life to atoms and to simple energy factors to the same extent that we can do this for chemistry and for physics.

It is not a peculiarity of physiology that the specific properties of an organism cannot be explained on the basis of structure and chemical composition. For instance, in chemistry, the properties of a compound are the result of the constituent atoms and their type of bonding; yet, the knowledge of a chemical structure is not enough to predict the properties of a substance (1897, p.4).

It is evident that Pfeffer's goal was today's molecular biology. He wanted to relate physiological phenomena to atomic and molecular processes. In proposing this, he differed fundamentally from most biologists of his time. While many of his contemporaries rejected vitalism as an explanation of physiological phenomena, they did not see — in the radical way that Pfeffer — did the multitude of these phenomena as the starting points for the investigation of molecular fundamentals. It was his goal to understand the "protoplast."

d) Biological Structures Do Not Have Sharp Boundaries. There Is No "Realization of an Idea"

Pfeffer's basic concept is illustrated by the following. At the occasion of his *Habilitation* examination [to be admitted to the faculty as a lecturer] in 1871, he had to present and defend two theses.[9] The first of these was entitled: "Root, Shoot, Leaf and Hair Are Not Sharply Separated Organs, Rather, They Are Connected with Each Other by Transitional Forms." The title of the second thesis was: "For the Relative Position of Plant Organs, Rules Probably

Apply in the Majority of Cases; However, There Are no General Laws." Pfeffer was addressing an important question. The theses were a challenge to many morphologists at the time, and a challenge even to some morphologists of our century. In Germany, the concept of an "ideal morphology" was very popular. Morphological concepts were seen as a "thought" of nature. Speemann defined the concept of an ideal morphology (to which he did not subscribe) in this way:[10] "The type was . . . an idea . . . a blueprint which in nature is used in the creation of organisms, and an image of a thought which makes the knowing spirit, retroactively, follow the way of nature." Furthermore, according to this philosophy of nature, everything was to be explained in set numerical proportions from the order in the planetary system to the order in the shape of plants. Pfeffer stressed that the organism is not a closed system in physiology (cf. p. . . .), and he held the same opinion regarding the morphology of plants.

These kinds of disputes may sound strange to present-day scientists. A "romantic philosophy of nature" no longer exists. It may be appropriate to recall that philosophers like Schelling, Oken and Hegel were much in fashion in Germany well into the nineteenth century. This was not the case in France and England. Schelling said that Bacon, Newton and Boyle were "perverting natural sciences," and Hegel derided scientists who performed experimental work. Only a concrete system of concepts was said to be of use. In Germany, a decisive change from the "romantic philosophy of nature" came about in the mid-nineteenth century. Yet the old way of thinking persisted for some time. It was typical for Carl Nägeli when asked to review the "laws" of Gregor Mendel (more than thirty years before they were rediscovered), to write that these results were "only empirical, not rational."[11] Nägeli had been "indoctrinated" by Hegel, but refused to admit it. His emancipation from the romantic philosophy of nature to scientific investigation was incomplete. Faced with these opinions, Pfeffer felt the need to present his first thesis. Nageli wanted to formulate "absolute concepts," and he stressed that there could be no "transitions" in morphology. We may summarize: Pfeffer, in a logical manner, advocated experimental research, free of preconceptions. Religious dogmas were not a part of his philosophy of life. He did not deny the existence of an "ultimate reason"; yet, his agnostic-sounding remark on the topic (cf. beginning of the chapter) corresponds to the view of life that his contemporaries attributed to him.

In his funeral oration, the pastor of the Reformed Church spoke at length about Pfeffer's character and his life. He also spoke about his human kindness, but he made no mention of a religious faith.[5]

3
PHARMACY - CHEMISTRY -
BOTANY - PHYSIOLOGY -
CELL BIOLOGY -
MOLECULAR BIOLOGY

a) In the Pharmacy

With his many talents, Pfeffer could have become not only a botanist or a zoologist, but just as readily a physicist, a chemist or an engineer. He became a botanist thanks to certain influences in his youth.

Pfeffer was born on March 9, 1845 in Grebenstein near Kassel; more specifically, he was born in the pharmacy his father had taken over from the grandfather, and the grandfather from the great-grandfather (fig. 1). He had a private tutor from the age of six to the age of twelve. He then attended the "Kurfürstliche Gymnasium" in Kassel for three years. At age fifteen, it was time to leave school and start an apprenticeship in his father's pharmacy. This was a thorough training, and it included the menial tasks which formed a part of the apothecary business. A friend of Pfeffer's youth, W. Stippel (an apprentice in the same pharmacy) relates:

> All medicinal preparations were made on the premises. In addition, it was typical for small country

15

Fig. 1 Portal of the pharmacy in Grebenstein. In 1955, a plaque was installed which reads: "In this house was born on March 9, 1845 *Geheimrat* [Privy Councillor] Professor Dr. Pfeffer. He investigated the nature of plants and recognized the laws of their existence." — Photo: Hermann Augustin, present owner of the pharmacy.

pharmacies to make chocolates, barley sugar, sugar-coated almonds, and marshmallow paste. Young Willi Pfeffer had to work his way up from the bottom, but in his later years this stood him well. The pharmacy was heated by a steam boiler which he had to start up and keep firing. He was also responsible for washing and cleaning cooking vessels, filter cloths and the like. Every Saturday, his job was to wipe off all containers and to polish the counters and the prescription table of the pharmacy. The polishing was done with a paste especially formulated for this purpose. In those days, it was not yet customary to obtain drugs in cut and powdered form; thus, he spent hours cutting roots and herbs, and pulverizing dried drugs with a heavy pestle in a mortar.[75]

At the age of eighteen, Pfeffer passed the examination for apothecary's assistant, and he started to study chemistry at the University of Göttingen (even though he had not continued high school to matriculation). At first, his intention was to become better equipped for the profession of apothecary. After only four semesters of study, at age twenty, he presented his doctoral thesis. The misgivings of several faculty members as to so short a time of study were dispelled by the excellence of his work.

Pfeffer continued his education as apothecary by studying one semester at the University of Marburg, and then by practicing as an apothecary's assistant, first in Augsburg and later in Chur. Pfeffer studied again in Marburg from 1868 to 1869, and there he passed the state examination in pharmacy.

b) Botanist

What was it that led Pfeffer to botany? The foundation was the influence of the environment of the pharmacy where his father had built up large collections of drugs, plants, shells and fossils. Already at the age of six, Wilhelm Pfeffer started collecting plants and animals. Thanks to the guidance of a distant relative, a professor at the "Kanton" school of Chur, Pfeffer — now twelve years old — learned to love the Alps and to know their geology and botany. In the Alps he became familiar with plants; he even planned a special study of the mosses of the Canton of Graubünden. Evidence of this intent are the papers he published in the four years after he obtained his Dr. Phil. degree. Several studies on the history of the development of morphology also fit the image of a classical botanist.

Pfeffer evolved from being a collector in his youth to an observer of processes of development, and then to the analyst studying causality. This development was typical for many biologists in the last century and in the first decades of this century (cf. p. 23). Although it was said that he had little respect for branches of botany not connected with plant physiology, Pfeffer never concealed his knowledge of plants. He demonstrated this knowledge while he was an apothecary's apprentice and was called upon to guide a tour as a substitute for a botanist from the University of Göttingen. Later, on field trips with his students, he easily identified higher and lower plants, as well as insects. For him, this was not a science but rather, a hobby. He also administered the botanical garden and its greenhouses with great diligence.

c) Physiology

It was Julius Sachs, the acknowledged founder of plant physiology, who showed Pfeffer the path to physiology. At the instigation of Sachs, Pfeffer undertook his first, purely physiological investigation, which dealt with the effect of different colours of light on the assimilation of carbon dioxide (1871c). In the end, Pfeffer went further than Sachs. Sachs treated plant physiology as an area of botany which had been neglected up to this point. He introduced the use of hydroponics, and he dealt with the physiology of germination, of roots, of stimulation, and with photosynthesis. He thus gave a significant impetus to the further research of these processes. These phenomena were also of interest to Pfeffer, but to him, they were primarily keys to the solution of general problems of biology. It may be said of Sachs and of many other outstanding biologists that they investigated separate subject areas with success. At the risk of oversimplification, it may be said of Pfeffer that he investigated diverse areas with the objective of finding as many starting points as possible to penetrate the molecular foundations of life's processes. "The expansion of our horizon to see a multitude of phenomena is one of the most important tools for gaining an ever deeper insight" (1893d). Hans Kniep accurately acknowledged this when speaking at the occasion of Pfeffer's seventieth birthday: "It is not possible to characterize the contents of Pfeffer's works with a few catchwords, and therein lies their significance. Individual problems are never treated in isolation; rather, basic principles constitute the starting point and the final goal. And another thing, it is not possible to classify his works into categories like the physiology of stimulus and other topics.[1]

As previously stated, Pfeffer's goal was to investigate the protoplast — the "elementary organism." He wrote:

> Every manifestation of life can invariably be traced back to the protoplast, that is to say, to a living elementary organism. Therefore, it is the task of physiology to explain the workings of this elementary organism by means of its properties and the functioning of its constituent parts.

19

The potential for every kind of life form lies dormant in the various species of the genus protoplast. Individual functions become more pronounced with their progressive development and their specialization, or these functions only become possible as the result of greater differentiation. With the adaptation to a specific primary function, the associated processes become clearer, and they are less clouded by other activities of the living organism. Therefore, the study of such specialized processes is of eminent significance, and it is an important tool for gaining an insight into the workings of the protoplast. With this goal in mind, it is of great significance that even unicellular organisms have capabilities and functions which are developed in a specific way, and which show very different characteristics (1897).

This explains why Pfeffer started early to include single-celled organisms in his research. Subsequent developments in biology fully bore him out, although it took decades for the acknowledgement of this to come about. As an example, long before the advent of the modern genetics of bacteria, Pfeffer made the following statement in the chapter "Variations and Heredity" of his *Pflanzenphysiologie*:

Our knowledge about the origin and the cause of variations will no doubt be increased with our present experience in physiology, and especially by making use of lower organisms with a short life-span. With this improved tool, we may hope to gain a better understanding of the variations which (in the sense of evolutionary teaching) led to the mighty armies of species — those which once existed and those which still exist today (1897).

He understood the difficulties that lay ahead, and wrote:

A watch ceases to be a watch when it has been crushed, yet the composition and the quantity of the metal is unchanged. Similarly, when we crush a slime-mould, the life of any protoplast and anything connected with it is irretrievably destroyed; yet, in this mixture the same substances are still present in composition and in quantity. This consideration leaves no doubt that even the best chemical knowledge of the components found in the protoplasm cannot be adequate to explain the vital processes. In the same way, a thorough chemical knowledge of coal and iron is not enough to understand the steam engine and the printing press driven by it (1897).

d) Molecular Biology, Micelles, Macro-Molecules

Molecular biology is concerned with research into the role of key molecules for the physiological processes. A typical example of modern molecular biology is the investigation of molecules which carry genetic information. This includes research on the structure, the functioning, and the duplication of the molecules. Modern membrane research is also a part of molecular biology, and Pfeffer's contributions to the investigation of the plasma membrane are beginnings in this field. From the analysis of his experiments on the structure of the *Plasmagrenzschicht* [plasma-margin layer, he concluded that its basic units are combinations of molecules rather than just single molecules. He called them tagmas (tagma: Greek, a heap in an orderly arrangement). This corresponded to some degree to Nägeli's concept of the "micelle."[13] "In any event, the micellar hypothesis is best suited for tracing physiologically significant events back to the molecular domain" (1897, p.68).

After Nägeli and Pfeffer, developments went a step beyond tagmas and micelles with the discovery of the giant molecules or macro-molecules. It must be added that in the first decades of this century, the concepts of these founders of the micelle theory were taken into consideration only in a fragmentary manner. The concept of the micelles evoked the idea of independent, large particles (somewhat like small crystals), or of aggregates of hundreds or thousands of molecules. Micelles were compared to colloids as they occur in soap. Around 1920, it was first reported that many molecules had been found to be linked by valence bonds. This was the start of macro-molecular chemistry, and its founder, Hermann Staudinger was later awarded the Nobel Prize.[13] Macro-molecules were found, and we now know that they can reach the size of a cell. For instance, the cell membrane of a bacterium cell may be a single macro-molecule (called murein). This macro-molecule is flat in shape, and it does not have the pronounced three-dimensional form that had originally been postulated for micelles. Here, again, is something Pfeffer had already thought of! "Para-tagma specifically describes a mass which exists predominantly in one plane" (1877a, p.32). Incidentally, Nägeli already had conceived of rows of micelles which can grow together. Pfeffer brought the concept of the micelle even closer to that of the macro-molecule: "There is no reason why . . . micelles should not reach a visible size . . . On the other hand, it is obvious that the protoplasm which is composed of distinct organs and elements of organs cannot be a single molecular complex; that is, it cannot be a homogeneous macro-molecule" (1897!).

e) Only a Laboratory Botanist?

Pfeffer performed his duties as *Ordinarius* [full professor] of Botany fully and conscientiously, in spite of his special interest in cell physiology and molecular biology. Many

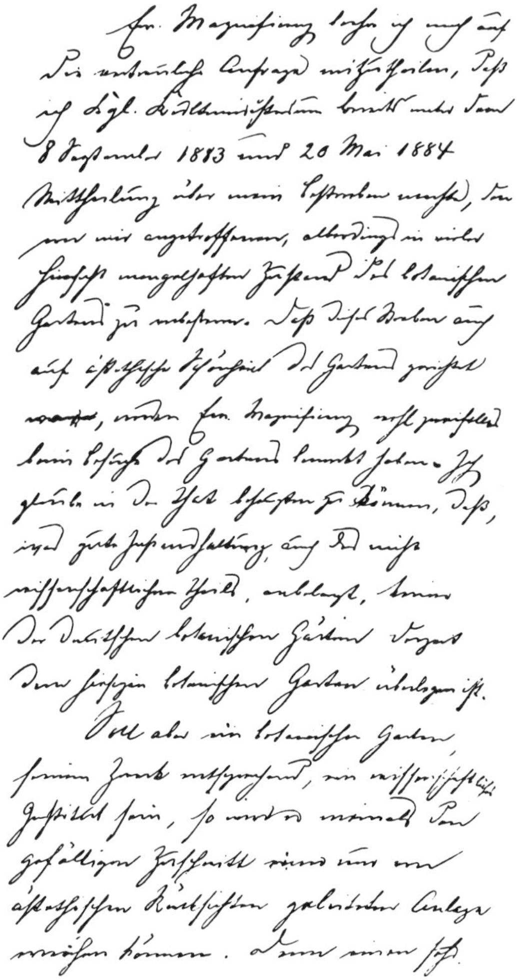

Ew. Magnificenz beehre ich mich auf
Die verehrliche Anfrage mitzutheilen, daß
ich dem Kgl. Cultministerium bereits unter dem
8 December 1883 und 20 Mai 1884
Mittheilung über mein Bestreben machte, den
von mir angetroffenen, allerdings in vieler
Hinsicht mangelhaften Zustand des botanischen
Gartens zu verbessern. Daß dieses Streben auch
auf ästhetische Schönheit des Gartens gerichtet
~~[illegible]~~, werden Ew. Magnificenz wohl zweifellos
beim Besuche des Gartens bemerkt haben. Ich
glaube in der That behaupten zu können, daß,
insofern gute Instandhaltung auch den nicht
wissenschaftlichen Theil anbelangt, keiner
der deutschen botanischen Gärten [illegible]
dem hiesigen botanischen Garten überlegen ist.
Soll aber ein botanischer Garten,
seinem Zweck entsprechend, ein wissenschaftlich
geschickter sein, so wird er niemals den
gefälligen Zuschnitt einer nur von
ästhetischen Rücksichten geleiteten Anlage
erreichen können. Denn einem sch.

Fig. 2 Extract from a letter of June 19, 1885 written by Pfeffer to the President of the University of Tübingen concerning the building of a greenhouse (the scientific purpose and the aesthetic considerations are pointed out). — Archives, University of Tübingen.

letters in the archives of the University of Tübingen testify to this. Here is just one example. Several new, beautiful and relatively large greenhouses were erected during Pfeffer's term of office. This came as a surprise to those who thought of him as a one-sided plant physiologist — a laboratory botanist who supposedly scorned other fields of botany. The records show that Pfeffer's predecessor, Wilhelm Hofmeister had requested that the old buildings be replaced, and he had filed a blueprint for this purpose, but it was rejected. Ten years later, Pfeffer submitted a new plan which was much more modest and was to cost only half as much as the Hofmeister proposal. In his submission, Pfeffer noted several times that the purely scientific needs called for only a small expenditure; however, "aesthetic considerations" should also be taken into account (fig. 2). He attached a rough draft of the proposed structure with his submission. In the end, in 1885, a more elaborate complex than the one Pfeffer had asked for was built, and in addition, his "aesthetic considerations" had been taken into account. When the botanical garden was relocated 85 years later, there was a great public effort to preserve the greenhouses (fig.3), but to no avail. The greenhouses were looked upon as heritage structures because they were precursors of modern steel and glass construction, and a testimony to a period in which the bourgeoisie introduced its own architectural styles in place of the symbols of the other classes.[14]

Pfeffer took good care of the botanical garden, even though this was an added responsibility to his work in research. "Not only did he perform his duties faithfully until the end, he even planned for the future good of the institute beyond his own life."[15] Pfeffer loved the botanical garden. It "revealed much of his personal, human affection; it was his garden, in which every plant along the path would seem to speak of the patriarchal gardener who loved them all and tended to their needs."[5]

Fig. 3 The completed building — an early example of modern steel and glass construction. Photo by Manfred Grohe, 7402 Kirchentellinsfurt.

4
MIMOSA, STAMINAL FILAMENTS, OSMOMETER, PLASMA MEMBRANE

a) From Staminal Filaments to the Osmometer

Osmosis is diffusion in a solution in the presence of a semi-permeable membrane. Semi-permeable membranes allow water to pass through with relative ease, while substances dissolved in the water either do not pass or pass only poorly. Dutrochet, a plant physiologist, discovered the significance of osmosis, and in 1828, built the first endosmometer (fig.6).[19] However, it was Pfeffer who eventually discovered the very high pressures associated with osmosis.

Pfeffer's osmotic investigations are an outstanding example of successful scientific research. Experimental skill, combined with logical thinking and planning, led to results of major importance.

The osmotic investigations had their start in experiments in plant movements such as the well-known leaf movements of *Mimosa*. Pfeffer had used *Mimosa* before in other experiments,[16] but he eventually used less complex organisms in his work. The stamens of the species *Centaurea jacea* (cf. fig. 4) were found to be suitable. It was known

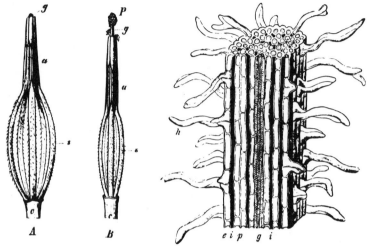

Fig. 4 Left: Flower of *Centaurea jacea* after the corolla has been removed, exposing the five staminal filaments. The stamens are shown at A in the unstimulated, at B in the stimulated condition (magnified about 5 X). filaments (s); tube formed by filaments growing together (a); corolla tube (c); stigma (g); pollen exposed at the apex after contraction of the stamen (p). Copied from Pfeffer's original drawing.
Right: A portion of the longitudinal half of a filament of *Centaurea montana* (magnified more than above).
vascular bundle (g); parenchyma (p); epidermis (e); intercellular spaces (i); hairs (h). From Pfeffer's original drawing.

that these filaments could contract, and the accepted explanation was that this was comparable to the contraction of a muscle. Pfeffer made exact measurements of the changes in length and thickness of the staminal filaments, and he recognized that a change in volume was involved. Therefore, the changes in the thickness of the stamen did not result from a contraction. In addition, he noted that a reduction in volume coincided with an outflow of water (to the extent that water was injected into the intercellular spaces which normally contain air). Pfeffer concluded that the movements were due to osmotic forces. The renewed expansion of the cells which had contracted when stimulated was the result of an endosmotic absorption of water.

Pfeffer continued his experiments by hanging weights from the contracting stamina to find out what "force" was needed for an expansion to take place without osmosis. The values found were much higher than seemed possible in the light of the then current knowledge about osmosis. Pfeffer's conclusion was: "We do not know enough about osmosis."

> When I tried to relate certain occurrences in movement to the underlying cell mechanism, I encountered significant facts which needed to be explained before any real advances in knowledge could be expected. Above all, it had to be determined how the surprisingly high hydrostatic pressure in plant cells could occur, even though the cell liquor represents only a dilute solution. The formulation of questions for subsequent scientific research was based on observations within the plant cell. The first step was to determine what osmotic pressures are exerted by dissolved substances, and especially by the so-called crystalloids, when they do not diosmose [do not pass through the membrane]. Precipitation membranes of the kind made by Traube were used to simulate the cell of a plant and to construct the apparatus for that part of the study which deals with questions of physics.[17]

The Traube precipitation membrane consists of copper ferrocyanide. It forms readily on a surface of a crystal of potassium ferrocyanide when the crystal is put into a dilute solution of copper sulphate. The membrane of copper ferrocyanide is semi-permeable, and it expands rapidly to a so-called Traube cell. Inside the membrane is a concentrated solution of potassium ferrocyanide which has a strong osmotic force. It cannot diffuse outward through the semi-permeable membrane; however, water from the dilute copper sulphate solution is absorbed inwards. When the skin bursts with expansion, a new membrane is quickly formed. Thus, the cell continues to "grow," and it can reach a length of several centimetres (fig. 5).

Is this an "artificial cell"? Of course not, if we think of it as a model of a living cell. Sachs[18] strongly rejected the idea of any such comparison. It remained for Pfeffer to uphold the comparison of the Traube cell with the living cell as it relates to a small and yet significant point — the semi-permeable membrane of the Traube cell is comparable to the membrane of the living cell to the extent that it allows water to pass inward easily, while practically all the solute in the cell is retained.

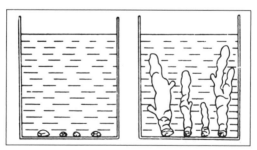

Fig. 5 Traube Cells. Crystals of potassium ferrocyanide are put into a solution of copper sulphate (left) and cells grow out of the solution (right). Copied from H.Walter, *Grundlagen des Pflanzenlebens*, 3rd ed. (Stuttgart: E. Ulmer, 1950).

Pfeffer's next step was to construct an osmometer, and in this he showed his skill as an experimenter. The floating Traube cell was not suitable. The membrane had to be held by a surface that was strong enough, and that would also allow the passage of water and salts. After many trials, a porous battery cell [Leclanché] or porous pot was found to

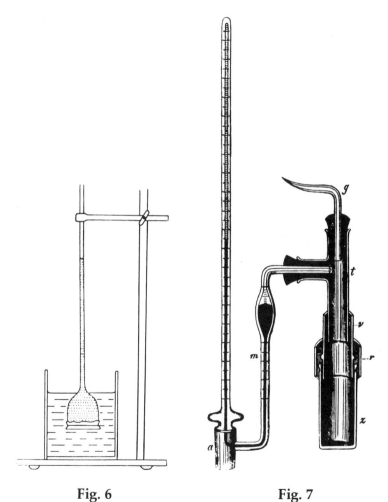

Fig. 6   Fig. 7

be most suitable. A semi-permeable membrane of copper ferrocyanide was made to adhere to the inside of the porous pot (fig. 7).

In 1875, Pfeffer described the results of his work to the *Niederrheinische Gesellschaft für Natur-und-Heilkunde* and to the forty-eighth meeting of the Society of German Naturalists and Physicians held in Graz.

Pfeffer tried over and over again before he was able to find a really usable type of porous pot. As an aside, he says in a footnote (1875d), "Most of the porous pots proved to be useless, and I had a great deal of trouble before I found a satisfactory material." That later researchers had great difficulty in making osmometers of the same quality is proof of his experimental skill. It took H. N. Morse (Baltimore) nearly fifteen years of effort before he could report on the construction of a better osmometer.[19]

Fig. 6 *(See previous page)* Diosmometer of Dutrochet. In the glass bulb is a sugar solution; in the surrounding container is water. A (semi-permeable) pig's bladder separates the two solutions. The water column rises because the sugar solution "sucks in" the water as the result of "osmotic pressure." After H. Walter (cf. fig.5).

Fig. 7 *(See previous page)* Osmometer (after Pfeffer's original drawing). Major components: The porous pot (z) which is about 46 mm high and the manometer (m). In his early experiments, Pfeffer worked with membranes that had been precipitated within the wall of the pot. This was achieved by filling the porous pot with a potassium ferrocyanide solution, and then immersing the pot into a solution of copper sulphate. The two compounds diffuse towards each other and react to form copper ferrocyanide as a precipitation membrane within the wall of the porous pot. In his main investigations, however, Pfeffer used membranes that had been deposited on to the inner wall of the pot. These "surface" membranes were formed first, by filling the porous pot with copper sulphate, next, by rinsing it quickly with water, and finally, by adding a solution of potassium ferrocyanide.

Using his osmometer, Pfeffer was able to prove that osmotic pressures were much higher than had been assumed before that time. It is of interest to note that the famous physicist, Clausius, remained skeptical. In a letter written to Cohen in Utrecht in 1910, Pfeffer says:

> I discussed the subject with Clausius, and at first he declared that such high pressures were impossible. After I gave a demonstration of the pressure experiments, he finally acknowledged the facts, although grudgingly. This may explain why Clausius did not involve himself with the subject any further, even though I repeatedly pointed out to him that there seemed to be an evident connection between osmotic forces on the one hand, and the size and numbers of molecules on the other hand.[20]

Pfeffer's experimental results became the foundation stone of van't Hoff's Theory of Solutions. In his acceptance speech for the Nobel Prize, van't Hoff specifically acknowledged the pioneering accomplishment of Pfeffer. The significance of Pfeffer's findings in the fields of biology and medicine is well known to college students in these subjects. The existence of a plasma membrane is also something every student knows about. It is less well known, however, that before Pfeffer, the fundamental need for such a membrane had barely been recognized.[21]

b) The Plasma Membrane

The expression *Plasmahaut* or *Plasmamembran* [plasma membrane] did not originate with Pfeffer. At first the expression had a different meaning, and W. Hofmeister (1867) gives the earlier meaning as follows:

> Every plasma mass is bounded on the outer surface by a thin layer which in certain cases has a measurable diameter. This layer is distinguished from the inner

mass in that it does not consist of the same large, solid and granular matter; furthermore, it is more translucent, shows a higher refraction for light, and has a greater density and firmness. This peripheral, skin-like layer of the protoplasma has no defined inner boundary ... The thicker outer layer of the proto-plasma shall be called its *Hautschicht* [skin layer].[23]

As early as 1877, Pfeffer was very specific in stating that his own concept of a plasma skin or plasma membrane did not agree with that of the Hofmeister *Hautschicht* (cf. fig. 17).

Textbooks make mention of the semi-permeable plasma membrane only after the studies of Pfeffer and de Vries[21] became known; even then, there remained well-known doubters for many decades. (cf. p. 8).

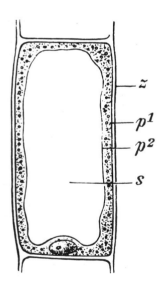

Fig. 8 Drawing by Pfeffer (here slightly enlarged) of a fully developed plant cell. (Except for the definition of the membranes, the drawing does not vary from that of other researchers). Pfeffer's accompanying text (1897): "In order to reach the cell-sap, a particle of water or a dissolved substance must diosmose first through the cell wall (z) and the adjoining *Hautschicht* (p^1), and finally through the membrane of the vacuole (p^2) which isolates the protoplasma from the cell-sap." (Equivalent terms used today: (z)= cell-wall, (p^1)=plasmalemma, (p^2)= tonoplast. Enlargement about 500 times).

Pfeffer did not only postulate the existence of a plasma membrane, but he also tried to prove his theory through experiments. The one objection he continued to run into was that these were pathological phenomena related to the dying of the cell. This argument continued even after de Vries came forward with more convincing experiments about the existence of the inner plasma membrane (he called it tonoplast) which separates the protoplast from the vacuole. It was not until after 1930, but before the use of the electron-microscope, that advanced experimental proof was finally available for the theses of Pfeffer and de Vries. Concerning the thickness of the plasma membrane, Pfeffer held that it was definitely a mono-molecular structure. In the end, it turned out that he had been close to the truth.

c) The Contractile Cell

Osmosis was not the only subject of interest which arose in the study of *Mimosa* and of certain stamens. Authors before Pfeffer had assumed that the movements of plants were the result of changes in the shape of the tissue — a contraction and not a change in volume. The comparison with the contraction of a muscle suggested itself easily. This view continued even after Pfeffer had announced his precise measurements, and he finally put out a strong statement: "As much as I regret to pass harsh judgment on the works of others, I consider it advisable not to remain silent when inaccuracies, ignorance and a lack of critical thinking are unfortunately manifest to such an inexcusable extent in these questionable works" (1875 a).

For many decades, there remained doubters that the movement of plant organs was caused by a loss of water with a related reduction in tension of the cell membrane. As late as 1937, sixty-four years after Pfeffer's findings, a book in a reputable scientific series completely rejected Pfeffer's conclusions and instead reverted to the comparison with a contraction of a muscle.[22] The book states, "This great plant physiologist makes the error that he will not recognize anything but his own ideas .... Thus, the research of others was overshadowed by the colossal authority of Pfeffer, and their voices were heard only much later."

Decisive advances in this area have been made only since the advent of more modern methods. Pfeffer's observation of the escape of water and other substances following mechanical stimuli can now be proven using the new techniques. Even so, the underlying cause remains unknown. In 1904, Pfeffer wrote: "We do not know the cause of this lowering of the osmotic pressure." Today, we still must accept the statement by Sibaoka: " . . . the central problem concerning the mechanism of the rapid movements — what occurs as the first mechanical change in the motor cells — is still far from a solution."[22]

Recent studies give some interesting new leads. The basic flows of ions in plants have been analysed, and the results show a certain parallel with the results of the studies on the effect of stimuli in animal cells. This would seem to support the objections against Pfeffer's idea about a difference between plant movements and the movements of muscles. However, the modern ion flow studies deal with a different dimension than the one Pfeffer dealt with in his studies of molecular-sized plasma membranes.

5

THE PLASMA MEMBRANE — "THE GATE KEEPER IN THE SERVICE OF THE PROTOPLAST"

a) Properties of the Plasma Membrane

Many of Pfeffer's contemporaries did not understand the objectives for his *Osmotische Untersuchungen* [*Osmotic Investigations*] and his reasons for postulating a plasma membrane. He was thought of as a scientist belonging to a large group that considered the Traube cell as a model for a living cell. It was believed he had gone too far in comparing the plasma membrane to the lifeless precipitation membrane. The polemic went as far as to say, "A membrane that is not visible is not a membrane."[23] On this subject, Pfeffer wrote:

> My concern with the question of the membrane as a separate part of the living protoplasma, and my use of the artificial precipitation membrane have given rise to many misunderstandings. This happened in spite of my emphasizing repeatedly that a study of physiological functions which are a known reality does not have to touch on the origin and the genetic relationship of the plasma membrane. In fact, I used

no other research methods than those available to investigate physiological questions. With these methods, I have clearly explained the manner in which the plasma membrane acts as the servant of the living protoplasm. The experiments with artificial precipitation membranes allowed me to give a physical explanation of how the high osmotic pressures which were discovered in my earlier investigations could also occur in living cells, even though the cell sap is only a dilute solution (1890c).

In summary, Pfeffer recognized that the plasma membrane is physically and chemically different from the rest of the protoplasm, and that it is also different from an artificial precipitation membrane. Yet, Pfeffer did not have the same concept as Hugo de Vries. In 1885, de Vries suggested the plasma membrane was of homogeneous origin, meaning it was formed by reproducing itself in the same manner as the cell nucleus and the chromatophores do.[24] Pfeffer did not agree, and he provided clear proof that a new plasma membrane is created where required from the cytoplasm (1890c). He never thought of the plasma membrane as simply comparable in all its physical properties to a copper ferrocyanide precipitation membrane. He visualized the plasma membrane as being "a living organism belonging to a living protoplasm complex" (1890c), and that "its location allows it to adjust the exchange of matter with the outside world" (1886a). In his investigations, Pfeffer also made it clear that uptake and exchange of matter were not related to the size of the molecules. He was cautious in his comments on the composition of the plasma membrane. He thought that proteins (albumins) were probably involved, but at the same time he was forceful in rejecting the notion that a minute film of oil was present. A rejection of the concept of the oil film was not a small matter in his day. It was generally assumed that there existed a molecule of oil at the surface of the protoplasm just as in the case of water and oil (1886a, 1890e).

Pfeffer used vital staining with analine dyes to study the passage of matter through the plasma membrane and to investigate plant cell exchanges. The vital staining of plant cells had first been observed twenty years earlier. Heidenhain, in particular, made use of vital staining for animal cells. It was Pfeffer who introduced this method in his investigations of the plasma membrane and of plant cell exchanges. This in turn, stimulated further research into many other areas, such as the permeability of membranes, the acidity of protoplasm and vacuoles, the oxidation-reduction potential, and the migration of substances. Some 3,000 projects are listed in a 1968 synopsis on research involving vital staining and vital fluorescence staining of plant cells and tissues.[25]

It is interesting that already in 1876, Pfeffer stressed the likelihood that all living cells should be able to ingest solid bodies similar to the plasmodia of slime moulds and amoeba. His discovery that the plasma membrane had the ability to close a wound promptly led him to this conclusion. The wide occurrence of this type of ingestion of solid bodies has been proven only recently.

b) Advances and Reversals after Pfeffer. Membranes Play an Active Role

It has been a long road to modern membrane biology since Pfeffer's investigations pointed the way. A study of the fundamental chemical and physical structure of membranes has become possible only recently. It was also found that both proteins and lipids are involved in the membrane structure. As Pfeffer expected, membrane biology has become such an important field that it now has its own literature in books and periodicals.[26] It may be of historical interest to note that the impetus for a broader investigation of the role of lipids in plant and animal membranes came from a botanist, Ernest Overton.[27] In 1895, he reported that the ability of certain substances to permeate through a membrane was clearly related to their solubility in lipids. Overton concluded that lipids were present in the plasma membrane, and later research proved that this was so.

Like Pfeffer, Overton did not believe that the plasma membrane was simply a *Oelhaut* [skin of oil] or lipid film. In its original form, the lipid theory of permeability as it related to the penetration of substances into the cell was too one-sided. Pfeffer was of the opinion that more detailed studies would "certainly" show that many substances which are insoluble or only slightly soluble in fatty matter would easily enter the cell. "This expectation, like many other predictions of the great physiologist was eventually found to be a fact" (Lindforss[27]).

It is unbelievable that intensive research in permeability continued for more than fifty years after Pfeffer's *Osmotic Investigations*, and no heed was paid to his warning that a membrane should not simply be thought of as a sieve. He wrote:

> However, Traube was essentially wrong in his theoretical explanation of the actual diosmotic process. When he neglected the molecular forces that are active between the membrane on the one hand, and the solute and the solvent medium on the other hand, this scientist formed the incorrect view that the membrane simply acts as a sieve. To him, this meant that a relative measure of the size of the molecules in a solution could be obtained by determining whether different substances would pass or would not pass through a membrane (1877a, p.2).

When he used the term "molecular forces," Pfeffer was evidently thinking of forces of absorption.

In spite of Pfeffer's suggestions for further research into membrane permeability and in spite of his specific warnings, two other theories took hold. They were the ultra-filter theory and the rivalling lipid theory. The former held that the size of the molecules determines the ability of a substance to permeate, while the second theory held that the solubility of the substance in oils was the deciding factor. To satisfy certain experimental contradictions, both theories were combined in the so-called lipid filter theory. In the 1930s, P. R. Collander especially was involved in showing that plasma plays an active role after all. He also noted the adenoidal (glandular) activity of the protoplasm, a feature previously postulated by Overton. In all of these theories, any reference to Pfeffer's points and arguments was forgotten.[27]

Decisive progress was not made until the advent of modern membrane biology. The discovery of enzymes and the discovery of carrier molecules within the membrane are two examples. This confirmed what Pfeffer already had suggested as a possibility. He had written, "a substance may be chemically combined with structural particles of the plasma membrane and then be moved inward to be split off again" (1897, p.88).

The ground lost after Pfeffer was so extensive that scientists in recent times were left with ideas such as those expressed in 1973 by D. F. Hoelzl Wallach and H. G. Knüfermann in their book, *Plasmamembran*. They wrote: "The membrane should no longer be considered in the classical sense as a barrier against permeability from the outside; rather, it should be thought of as a switch board in which extra-cellular signals are converted to active intra-cellular messages."[26] Needless to say, this is the very way in which Pfeffer thought of membranes in the "classical" days!

Research into the structure of the membrane has not yet reached its conclusion. Different models have been constructed with the help of electron-microscopic and with physiological investigations. They all postulate the active participation of proteins (in line with Pfeffer's thinking) and of lipids (in line with Overton's thinking). Pfeffer suggested that proteins in the plasma membrane are a major component of the enzymes that control the absorption or excretion of substances. The modern models of membranes are a logical sequence to Pfeffer's experiments and thoughts.

The most recent models of the membrane do justice to everything that Pfeffer and later, Overton had stipulated. With the electron-microscope it was possible to show the existence of the plasmalemma and the tonoplast (fig. 8), and also to determine the existence of many intra-cellular membrane systems. Already, one hundred years ago, Pfeffer gave his reasons for suspecting this possibility: "... we should ask the question whether a plasma membrane encloses other substances made of protoplasm, such as cell nuclei or grains of coloured matter within the body of the protoplast, ... for several reasons this question is very important" (1877a). As evidence for his idea, he pointed to the finding that the nuclei of cells and chlorophyll grains (that is chloroplasts) which had been isolated and put into sugar solutions showed changes in volume, depending on the concentration of the solution. Consequently, they exhibit a "diosmotic behaviour."

Pfeffer's pre-eminence as a scientist is evident when one sees that it took many decades before researchers in membrane biology understood the significance of his experimental and intellectual analysis of the processes of the absorption of substances. He determined that the absorption of substances was not primarily a question of molecular size, and he spoke of "molecules being impelled to pass through" the membrane as the result of "molecular interaction between the membrane and the substance in solution" (1886a).

In the preceding few decades, the perception of a stimulus was thought to originate within the protoplasm. Today, the investigations of the fundamental process of perception of a stimulus generally point to the plasma membrane as the locus. When Pfeffer dealt with chemotaxis and chemotropism, he described the reaction of the outer membrane to a foreign contact as the "first act of perception" (1893d). Elsewhere he writes: "The autogenous or etiological changes in sensitivity indicate that the surface membrane must have a sensitivity (sensitivity structure) that is variable." Such formulations point in the same direction as the most recent views on the physiology of stimulus.

The function of membranes in receiving and processing signals is a major area of research in modern membrane biology. An early pioneer in this field is the famous Paul Ehrlich.

6

THE SINGLE-CELLED ORGANISM
HAS THE ABILITY TO DO
EVERYTHING. A FEW LETTERS
ARE ADEQUATE FOR
THE GENETIC CODE

Pfeffer's point of view can best be expressed with the above heading. Many people were shocked when in 1961, the Nobel Prize laureates J. Monod and F. Jacob put forward the axiom that everything that is found to be true for (the bacterium) *Escherichia* must also be true for elephants. But in fact this statement is only an extension of Pfeffer's clearly expressed opinion that all physiological achievements of higher organisms depend on cell functions already present in single-celled organisms. The only difference is that a higher organism achieves a greater degree of differentiation and the specialization of distinct organs for the fulfilment of certain functions. A "potential lies dormant" in every protoplast for any possibility (cf. p. 19,20).

Pfeffer made a continuous effort to prove that specific abilities of some plants are merely the result of the specialization of characteristics typical of all plants. In 1875, Darwin published a book on insect-eating plants, and many scientists assumed that this new kind of nutritional behaviour represented a special physiological principle. Pfeffer argued against this perception in 1877, showing that this was merely a specialization of the general manner in which plants absorb nutrition. Similarly, he explained that the clearly developed *Tastreizbarkeit* [sensitivity to touch] of twining plants is not unique to these plants, but it is present in many other varieties of plants. In his last published paper in 1916, he deals once more with the subject in detail. He discusses experiments undertaken in his laboratory by P. Stark and writes: "Based on this and other findings, we may assume that the property of sensitivity to touch exists quite extensively, although it is not as well developed" (as in twining plants). Today, we know that sensitivity to touch is one of the oldest phylogenetic senses; it is already present in bacteria.

Covering a broader area, Pfeffer wrote:

> It is sufficient to have a relatively small number of invisible physiological units . . . which shall generally be described as pangenes. In all cases, these are living units which combine in multiple ways to form units of a higher order. These latter units, in turn, combine into parts of organs and into organs. To get a clearer concept, it is useful to think of the letters of the alphabet. By combining letters into words and words into sentences, an unlimited number of combinations and thoughts can be formed. Also, the array of hydrocarbon compounds shows us the enormous number of substances that can be formed by the combination of three or four elements. In the same way, there should be no need to have a large number of pangenes to explain the immense magnitude of living structures, organs and living matter in general (1897, p.7).

This is almost a vision of the genetic code as we know it today. Four "letters" (bases) transmit all the required information in the deoxyribonucleic acid double helix.

Regardless of the complexity of the problem, Pfeffer always chose to use simple objects for his experiments. In his investigation of osmosis, he turned to the use of filaments of stamens after first using *Mimosa* (cf. p. 27). In resolving the processes of absorption of substances, he worked among other things with the plasmodia of slime moulds.[29]

As time progressed, he favoured the use of single-celled organisms in experiments, and his investigations on chemotaxis are an example of this approach (cf. p. 50).

7
SENSITIVITIES OF
SINGLE-CELLED ORGANISMS

If the study of the attraction of bacteria by oxygen is thought of as chemotaxis, then Theodor Engelmann is its discoverer. Chemotaxis in a broader context means the attracting or repelling effect on motile single-celled organisms by various substances which are in solution in the substratum. Chemotaxis in this sense was discovered simultaneously and independently by E. Stahl and W. Pfeffer.[30]

In 1884, and again in 1888, Pfeffer reported on the chemotaxis of the spermatozoa of ferns and mosses and on the chemotaxis of bacteria and flagellata.[30] The method used in the experiments was simple. The substance to be examined was put into capillary tubes that had been fused at one end. The open end of the capillary tube was inserted into drops of water containing micro-organisms. This was then studied under the microscope. In the case of positive chemotaxis, the micro-organisms accumulate around the mouth of the capillary tube and migrate into the tube (fig. 9). Pfeffer found that various organic and inorganic substances are attractants for certain bacteria and for colourless and green flagellata. In those days, it was a startling revelation that "already one part in a billion or

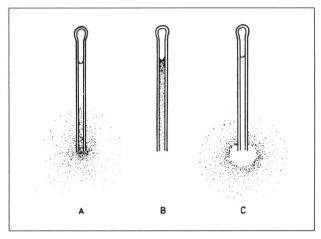

Fig. 9 Chemotaxis of bacteria. Capillary tube (A) contains a 1 per cent meat-extract in solution. Within a few minutes bacteria congregate at the mouth. Tube (B) contains an air bubble which also leads to an action of chemotaxis. Tube (C) contains a meat-extract made sour; the acid results in a repelling of the bacteria which congregate at a certain distance from the mouth of the tube. (According to Pfeffer's original drawing).

a trillion of one milligram" was enough to cause an attraction.[31] Pfeffer also confirmed the validity of Weber's law in these early studies. He wrote:

> The additional intensity of stimulus required to produce a perceptible reaction is proportional to the intensity of the existent stimulus. Until a threshold value is reached, the absolute difference between the contents of the liquid in the capillary tube and the liquid on the outside will increase as the amount of stimulant in the outside liquid becomes greater. It is concluded that a stimulant in homogeneous

distribution does not direct the movement of the organism; however, it does influence the perception of a stimulus by the organism (1884).

Today, Weber's law is not considered to be exact in its entirety, although some authors after Pfeffer still considered it to be so. No longer is any value given to speculations (of these, Pfeffer always disapproved) which went as far as to call the law a psycho-physical law. As far as Pfeffer was concerned, this was "a relationship which was only correct within certain limits" (1883d). Nevertheless, the discovery of the habituation effect and the resultant desensitization was of great importance for subsequent research. On Pfeffer's suggestion and under his direction, H. Kniep made use of the habituation effect to test whether bacteria have different degrees of chemical sensitivity. Should bacteria have only a single *Sinnesqualität* [type of sensitivity], then one substance should cause the same desensitization as any other substance. It was found that the assumption was incorrect; Kniep discovered three different types of perception in one kind of bacterium. Kniep found that the bacterium made a qualitative distinction between the amino acid asparagin, H-ions, and OH-ions. The results confirmed what Pfeffer had expected, and they agreed with his earlier analysis of data developed in 1888. At that time, he had concluded that there existed different processes of perception towards different substances; he compared these specific sensitivities with the stimulative effects of substances which humans perceive through taste.[33]

The whole question of the sensitivity of lower organisms was ignored for a long time after the early studies in Pfeffer's laboratory. Only recently, since about 1960 (!) has there been a renewed, successful investigation of the subject. Pfeffer's methods were again used in a modified way.[34] The new work examined in greater detail the faculty of discrimination in bacteria; at the same time, it showed that Pfeffer was correct when he wrote in reference to reception [term now used for perception] that there can be little doubt that the plasma membrane is involved in the process (1893d). J. Adler, proceeding from Pfeffer's method of experimentation, found eight separate chemoreceptors in *Escherichia coli*; of these, one or the other may be eliminated by mutation. He comments as follows:

> The availability of behavioral mutants of bacteria — for example, mutants of the types reported here — together with the existence of a great body of knowledge about the genetics and biochemistry of *Escherichia coli*, should make the bacterial system a favorable one for studying simple forms of behavior and perhaps even some primitive kinds of "learning" ... studies might emerge a set of facts and concepts that can be applied to investigations of more complex phenomena in higher organisms.

This agrees with the opinion Pfeffer expressed eighty years before when he wrote, "The entire secret of life and the specific sensitivities intertwined with it rest in the basic organism — the protoplasm. Therefore the sensitivity to stimuli is just as manifoldly and richly developed in the simple organism — be it a bacterium or a slime mould — as in any highly developed type of plant" (1893d).

As early as 1890, Pfeffer's method of studying chemotaxis was used to clarify pathological occurrences in humans. Then, after a pause of decades, it provided the starting point for new studies in other fields of science.

At the turn of the century several researchers, continuing the work of Pfeffer's school, studied the "behaviour of lower organisms." Thereafter, work with single-celled organisms was largely given up because it was thought that work with lower organisms could not be of much help with urgent problems, such as the problems in the physiology of the nerves. Now there has been a change — a return to Pfeffer. Today, it is being asked if single-celled organisms are better subjects than higher organisms for the study of phenomena of learning and memory.[36] There has been a logical continuation of the studies on the attracting and repelling effects of substances on bacteria which were started by Pfeffer, and it has been found that different receptors exist for these effects. A kind of "memory" exists which allows the organism to compare one chemical substance to another.[37] It is of interest to note that in the newer publications on this topic "Pfeffer, 1888" is regularly quoted, while practically all other references are from publications after 1960.

8
TRIGGERING WITHIN
THE ORGANISM

a) "Stimulation"

Today, the technical terms relay and relay-triggering are commonly understood. Biologists know that in physiology a process of stimulation simply means a process of triggering. In the previous century this was not yet a common concept.

Originally, the idea of a "stimulus" was closely related to psychic experiences of humans; the concept was eventually transferred to animals and then to plants. This led some authors to speak of psychic forces in the plant. They even cited Weber's law to support their idea because the term "feeling" was used in the original definition of the law.

Other authors rejected the whole concept of stimulation because they disagreed with the proposition that some mystical forces were at work. They searched for very simple explanations for plant movements. Thus, the outstanding plant physiologist de Candolle said in 1832 that a sensitivity could not be involved in phototropism and in geotropism because these types of plant movements could readily be shown to be of physical origin.[38]

Pfeffer took credit for being the first to publish (in 1877 and 1881) "a correct concept and appreciation of the nature and the general significance of the triggering processes within the workings of the organism" (1893d). He had, as he himself said, robbed the "stimulus" of its mystical aura, and he had brought back a clear concept of a mechanical release. He also emphasized the overall importance of triggering processes in all of the workings of the organism. In addition, he noted that triggering processes could be caused by internal factors and not only by external factors:

> When speaking of "stimulation," only the living organism is recognized as the seat of the trigger . . .. Thus, the concept of the stimulus is based purely on mechanical actions, and it can be as readily defined as the concept of the triggering. In regard to the organism, the following may be stated: a stimulation takes place when an external or internal impulse leads to given actions which are carried out by means available within the organism or by means attainable by the organism. With stimulation, new actions are brought about or actions already in progress are redirected . . . . In consequence, we include in the processes of stimulation all those activities which, in keeping with the characteristics of a trigger, serve the organism; this includes processes of metabolism and of energy exchange (1893d).

These conclusions were important for the development of plant physiology. Here as in other instances, Pfeffer made a point of making known his achievements and his claims of being the originator of certain concepts. This may seem surprising when compared to the manner of reporting new scientific discoveries today; however, it was a fairly common practice in Pfeffer's day. He did mention that scientists in animal and human physiology, in particular J. Mueller and duBois-Reymond, had already rejected the false concepts about a psychic stimulus. It may be noted that Pfeffer, even in his later statements on the subject, did not make reference to the relevant investigations of Robert Mayers.[39] Mayers was an advocate of the principle of the conservation of energy in biology; others used the phenomenon of triggering as an argument against this principle. In response, Mayer put out a special paper in 1876 (31 years after the publication of his book on the conservation of energy) on "Die Auslösung" [The Triggering] to explain that there are factors which may release energy which is present in latent form. He wrote: "Our entire life is tied to an uninterrupted process of triggering." In this connection, he also pointed to the process of fermentation and to the action of enzymes.

Pfeffer (1893d) stated that the physiologist "is not required" to deal with "the question of the extent to which plants and animals might be endowed with psychic emotions. . . . The results of the act of stimulation . . . cannot reveal whether any level of awakening consciousness has been reached . . . in the worm that twitches when touched or in the bacterium which hurries towards food". He illustrated this view by comparing "the haste with which a bacterium turns to food" with that of "the beast of prey bounding . . . towards the catch". Even after Pfeffer's clarifications, it was surprising that many biologists believed that the concept of a "stimulus" should be eliminated from physiology because it carried a "psychic connotation". They had not read his clarifications with care.

Pfeffer, having defined clearly what we know and what we do not know, did not hesitate to speak of "stimulation" and of "sensations," even for bacteria.

b) "Senses"

Pfeffer used various experiments to demonstrate the great difference in energy between the triggering agent and the reaction being released. Chemotaxis has already been mentioned in this connection. In another example, he investigated the bending movement of twining plants. He found that bending is already caused when a cotton thread as light as 0.00025 milligrams is placed on it.[40] Pfeffer concluded that the sensitivity of some twining plants exceeds the sensitivity of the skin of humans.

He proved that the plant can distinguish between stimuli caused by shaking or impact and those caused by gentle touch or contact. At least two different points on the surface of a twining plant must be touched before there is a successful stimulation caused by contact. Pfeffer pointed to the similarity of the conditions under which the human and the plant epidermis are affected by contact stimuli. He searched for and found the spots at which the plasma membrane moves close to the surface of the outer plant wall (fig. 10).

In his anatomical studies after 1896, G. Haberlandt explored in depth the similarity of the "sensory organs for

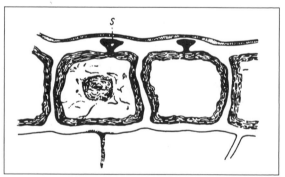

Fig. 10 *Fühltüpfel* [sensitive pits] (s) located in the sensitive surface of a pumpkin tendril. Copied from Pfeffer, 1885.

mechanical stimuli both in animals and in plants."[41] This entire problem has not been looked into again until fairly recently. Pfeffer's results did not have to be revised, but eventually there did occur a more extensive analysis of the individual processes.[42] Receptor cells for contact stimuli in plants and in animals have been found to show similar characteristics in tests which involved electro-physiology and the use of the electron-microscope. In all of this, endo-membranes (membranes within the plasma) clearly play a decisive role.

Pfeffer was always interested in the existence of different "sensitivities." He claimed that plants were no less endowed than animals. In connection with the question of the sensitivity of bacteria (cf. ch.7), attention is called to an investigation by Carl Correns. (Correns worked with Pfeffer in 1893-1894. He was one of the re-discoverers of Mendel's law, and he became famous for his work in genetics.) Correns proved that gravity-perception and photo-perception depend in different ways upon the concentration of oxygen, and therefore, different processes of perception must exist.[43]

In his last publication, Pfeffer dealt again with the question of "senses" (1916). He noted, for example, that the location of highest sensitivity to light in oat seedlings was found to be distinctly separate from the location of highest sensitivity to contact. These conclusions were based on research performed by P. Stark in Pfeffer's laboratory.

9
REGULATION AND FEEDBACK IN THE ORGANISM

a) Feedback, Law of Mass Action

Since the development of cybernetics, feedback has
become a widely accepted concept in modern biology. It is
a term which has been adopted from engineering, as were
many other terms and concepts of bio-cybernetics. The
principle of feedback was noted by some earlier biologists,
but it was most clearly formulated by the famous French
physiologist Claude Bernard.

Pfeffer stressed the great significance of the feedback
principle on many occasions. He wrote:

> The correlations and the other phenomena dealt with
> here are . . . only special cases of the greatly diversified
> regulatory processes that permeate and direct the
> whole mechanism of the plant. Without a functional
> self-regulatory control . . . a systematic growth
> pattern would be unthinkable; it would be impossible
> to achieve and maintain a harmonic interaction of the
> parts under changing conditions. In order for the
> plant to achieve self-regulation (as a mechanism and
> as an organism), the regulatory events must be
> triggered by the type and intensity of the events
> affecting it. This is the case when the plant is

maintaining equilibrium, when it undergoes progressive changes, when it experiences periodically recurring changes and so on. In other words, the response to a stimulus and to a need triggers the mechanisms to satisfy the need. Thus, consumption regulates the replenishment of nutrients, isolated shoots can develop roots as required, mechanical stress leads to an increase of the carrying strength of a shoot . . . One thing is certain, many different means and complex combinations serve to achieve the diverse types of regulation, and as mentioned earlier, the processes of stimulation play a major role in this. It can be shown that stimulation is often the result of some type of shortage or surplus; more generally, it may be seen as the result of an upset in balance. Hand in hand with the triggering mechanism, mass action plays a most significant role in carrying on the metabolic processes (1897).

Pfeffer investigated the significance of the law of mass action with respect to regulatory processes. In his laboratory, it was discovered that in an isolated maize endosperm (the reserve tissue within the ovule of the maize seed), sugar forms rapidly through the action of diastase (a starch hydrolyzing enzyme), only when the sugar is removed quickly as it is being produced. In the experiment, this was accomplished by attaching grains of endosperms to water-saturated plaster rods which were then placed in water. In this way, the isolated endosperms were subjected to similar conditions as are endosperms within the seed from which the embryo absorbs the sugar. In addition, it was found that the storage tissue of the endosperm can be reactivated to again take up sugar.[44]

b) Adaptation of Enzyme Formation to the Substrate

An interesting example of Pfeffer's studies of regulation is the adaptation of enzyme formation to the available substrate [enzyme induction. Some recent textbooks claim that this kind of adaptation has only been known since about 1955, and that its discovery was a result of modern work on the genetics of bacteria.

In fact, it was Pfeffer, who together with his students J. Katz and B. Hansteen, demonstrated that micro-organisms form specific enzymes in quite different amounts depending upon given circumstances. As an example, the mould *Penicillium glaucum* "does not make use of its ability to form diastase" when the sugar content in the nutrient solution exceeds 1.5%. Similar behaviour was found in the case of *Bacterium megatherium*.[44]

In these cases, as in later experiments with mushrooms in Pfeffer's laboratory, the adaptation of the enzyme to the substrate depended on the quantity of the specific enzyme involved. However, Pfeffer also suggested the possibility that completely new enzymes could be formed in the adaptation to specific substrates.[44] Today, the distinction is made between inducible enzymes and the ever-present constitutive enzymes.

The regulatory processes in metabolism were dealt with in other publications by Pfeffer and his co-workers. Some of this work was connected to the findings of Louis Pasteur who had discovered that mushrooms are able to distinguish between the two optically active types of tartaric acid during digestion. These kinds of investigations by Pasteur were later carried on by other researchers. Pfeffer understood the phenomena involved ("Über Elektiven Stoffwechsel," 1895e), and he related them to other features of selective metabolism. Thus, he found that glycerine is not removed from the nutrient substrate if glucose is also made available. In addition, he demonstrated that the substrate shows a preference for sugar over glycerine even though it is the glycerine that penetrates into the cell. Pfeffer always (starting with comments in his *Osmotische Untersuchungen*) gave special value to the law of mass action when he explained the concept of self-regulation in metabolism. At the same time, he emphasized that other very complex factors were involved, and it would "be difficult to throw light on them" (1897, p.520).

For the benefit of those who are not biologists, it should be added that now there exists a thorough understanding of the molecular mechanisms in the activation and in the inhibition of enzyme formation and also of the molecular mechanisms in the activation and the inactivation of constitutive enzymes. These advances in our knowledge had their origins in Pfeffer's "Ausblick auf Selbsteuerung" [Overview of the Process of Self-regulation], (1897).

c) Oscillations about Equilibrium

When working with regulators in technology, oscillations around the point of equilibrium are a common feature. Pfeffer drew attention to oscillations in organisms by comparing them to the swings observed in mechanics:

> The plant's reaction of bending usually goes beyond the point of equilibrium because of autogenous and endogenous factors and because of actions started by the movements; equilibrium is again established only after one or several oscillations .... When the thermostat is suddenly raised in a room, the air will heat up more rapidly than the mercury in the regulator, and the temperature in the room and the mercury column of the regulator will initially oscillate

widely around the equilibrium point. In the case of tropistic and nastic plant movements, as in other physiological reactions, oscillations of varying intensity around the final position of equilibrium are seen. One is dealing with the same kind of oscillations in the case of the after-effects of diurnal movements, although these oscillations persist for a longer time.[45]

The only sentence which Pfeffer later found to be incorrect is the last one (cf. p. 85).

10
ACTIVATION, REGULATION, FEEDBACK APPLIED TO THE TECHNOLOGY USED FOR PHYSIOLOGICAL STUDIES

It has already been noted that Pfeffer showed great talent and skill in performing his experiments. He developed many methods for these experiments, and he constructed many types of apparatuses which eventually were to be used throughout the world. If one were to list all the methods and experiments developed by Pfeffer and his students, it would result in a reference list of most of the multitude of experiments they undertook. Two examples will be given to illustrate how Pfeffer used the concepts of activation, regulation and feedback in developing his technological methods for the study of physiology, in the same manner that he used these concepts to explain the functioning of organisms.

Many research projects in plant physiology call for controlled temperature and light conditions. Today, electronically controlled climate chambers are common. Before Pfeffer's time, it was customary to use deep cellars, mines or caves. While it was possible to find relatively constant temperatures for experiments, there were obvious disadvantages. For example, temperatures were too low or they fluctuated during the course of a day. In 1893, Pfeffer constructed a constant temperature room in the Botanical Institute of Leipzig; it represented a good compromise between the old type of vaults and the controlled climate chambers of today (1895a). The temperature in this room varied markedly between the ceiling and the floor, but it varied by only 0.3°C at any given elevation. The many experiments Pfeffer completed under these conditions seem to prove that he had fewer vexations with his room than scientists have today with their modern controlled climate chambers (fig. 11).

A second example of Pfeffer's ingenuity is his device for an automatic regulation of illumination (1907a). Pfeffer used the just invented tantalum lamp as his light source. This apparatus allowed him to achieve a rapid or a gradual transition from light to dark and vice versa; and in addition, this could be done widely at varying intervals. The great range of successful experiments conducted with this apparatus testifies to the reliability of its construction (fig. 12).

The excerpts from the text accompanying figures 11 and 12 show how much thought must have gone into these constructions.

Devices such as those described were a sensation in their day. Other botanical institutes used regulated temperature experiments at a much later time, and these experiments were performed in vaults. The many smaller instruments, constructed or improved by Pfeffer, became standard equipment in botanical institutes in Germany and abroad. Soon, microscopes and microtomes were no longer the only instruments used in the laboratories. Already in his Tübinger days, Pfeffer received so many enquiries about equipment that he published a listing (1887).

Pfeffer made improvements, often very significant improvements, on numerous methods and devices already

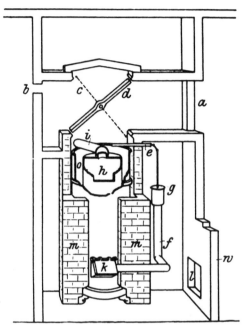

Fig. 11 Pfeffer's "constant temperature room." "The combustion heater which is housed in an antechamber supplies the heat; the wall (*w*) separates this from the test room. The hot air rising in the jacket of the heater (*o*) reaches the brick-lined chamber and from there — as long as the flap (*d*) is in the position shown in the illustration — passes through the opening (*a*) into the test room. Should the temperature there rise too much, the flap turns 90° (position *c*), and the hot air escapes through opening (*b*) into the chimney. To avoid too rapid a drop of temperature in the test room, provision is made to prevent the flap from closing too tightly in the (*c*) position, and to increase the supply of hot air to the test room by partly closing the opening (*b*). The electrical connection which causes the flap to turn, is initiated by a thermometer placed near the ceiling of the warming room and equipped with an adjustable contact. If this contact is interrupted, the flap is in the (*d*) position. When the circuit is

> closed, an electromagnet pulls the lever of a timing mechanism placed in an adjoining room, and the flap assumes the position (c). The heater opening (k) remains permanently closed; the combustion air is admitted through the duct (f) in conjunction with an adjustable opening at (g). The raising and dropping of the lid on opening (g) is activated by a metal thermometer (e), which protrudes from the brick-lined air chamber." [This text is copied from Pfeffer-Fest- paper, 1915. — Original: Pfeffer 1895a.]

---

in use. This applies to his micro-chemical investigations of protein granules (1872h), and it applies especially to his studies of the absorption of aniline dyes (1886a). In his studies of protein granules, he used micro-chemical methods with such previously unavailable precision that the expert micro-chemist Tunmann wrote: "The first outstanding achievement in the field of plant micro-chemistry was Pfeffer's investigation of aleurone granules."[46]

Just a perusal of the index of Pfeffer's publications shows how much he did both to improve existing methods of experimentation and to introduce new methods. For decades many of his methods continued to be used in plant physiology, in research, and in teaching. As an example, prior to Pfeffer's time, projectors were used mainly for showing lantern slides. Pfeffer thoroughly investigated and described how such equipment could be used in the lecture hall to demonstrate the movements of single-celled and higher organisms, as well as their reaction to stimulating effects. He also used the projector to demonstrate plasmolysis, the growth of the Traube cell, the assimilation of carbon dioxide, et cetera (1900).

Pfeffer did not build equipment purely for the pleasure of putting it all together. An accumulation of unused or seldom used equipment (as is so often the case today) did

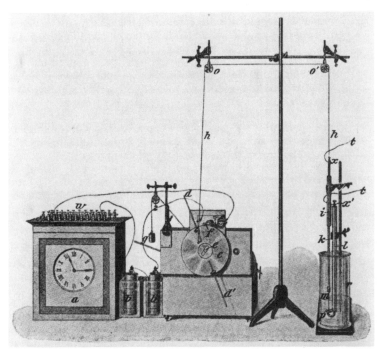

Fig. 12 Pfeffer's equipment for an automatically adjustable illumination.
"This equipment consists of a clock (*a*), which (with the use of 3
Leclanché batteries (*b*) . . .) closes a circuit, thereby lifting catch
(*f*), and thus causing disc (*c*) (which is attached to the drive shaft
of the clinostat) to make a half turn. As a result, string (*h*) which
runs over pulleys (*d*) and (*o'*) is raised or lowered, and it in turn
raises or lowers the glass tube (*k*) with the attached platinum rod
(*m*) within glass tube (*i*). The removal of the platinum rod from
the stationary platinum plate (*p*) interrupts the electrical circuit;
while the re-establishment of the platinum contact closes the
lighting circuit (*f*) and (*t*). Since the glass cylinder (*r*) contains a
solution of sodium sulfate, the gradual lifting of the platinum rod
(*m*) results in a greater resistance because of the higher column of
liquid, and this causes the lighting to dim gradually. The light is
completely extinguished when the platinum rod is lifted above

the solution. The opposite happens when the platinum rod is immersed: there is a gradual transition from darkness to a dawn-like light to a full illumination. It should be mentioned that the platinum rod (m) and platinum plate (p) are fused to the glass tubes (k) and (l), and some mercury has been poured into the tubes. A copper wire is dipped into the mercury making contact with the pole screws (x) and (x') which receive the lighting circuit wires (t) and (t'). The automatic release is transmitted by the clock (a) . . . The vertically placed disc (c) (attached to a shaft of the clinostat) has two notches at opposite sides of the rim into which the catch will drop when it is not held up by the electromagnet. In this way, the movement of the disc is stopped. Attached to the disc are two posts which receive rods (d) and (d'). One of them (d) has a stud at its end with an eyelet which rotates on its axis, and it has a string (h) attached to it. Varying the distance of the eyelet from the center of the disc permits the lift height of the platinum rod (m) to be changed, irrespective of a given angle of rotation of disc (c). Since the suspended glass rod (k) weighs about 35g, the lift load imposed on the clinostat is very small, and it can be further reduced by counterbalancing the moveable rod d' [if necessary through the use of a sliding balancing weight].
When the disc (c) is mounted on the different shafts of the clinostat which I also constructed, its rotation time can be varied from 2 minutes to 8 hours by means of 3 clinostat drive cones. The catch (f), together with its accessories, which is mounted on a plate can be attached in the required position for each of the three arrangements of the disc." From Pfeffer, 1907.

---

not exist in his laboratory. Pfeffer's co-workers always spoke of his frugality and of his scrupulously exact expenditures, which were limited to the true necessities.

11
ENERGETICS

a) There is no Special Vital Force

As noted on page . . . ., Pfeffer started from the premise that the law of the conservation of energy was generally valid for plant physiology. He and several other physiologists were firmly convinced of the correctness of this premise. The experimental proof was eventually supplied by Z. Rubner in 1894 — two years after Pfeffer's "Studium zur Energetik der Pflanzen" — using experiments in animal physiology.[47] Pfeffer had firmly rejected any idea that an organism may have special types of energy; he also affirmed that an organism has only those kinds of energy that are known for the inanimate world.[48]

Following the experiments on animals by Rubner and four years later by Laulané, and on humans by Atwater,[47] biologists no longer had any doubt that the law of the conservation of energy was valid for the processes of life. In spite of this, not only philosophers but also some well-known scientists, such as J. von Liebig and E. Pflüger, maintained that "living molecules" are distinct from dead molecules in that they have a higher energy content. In the end, it was experiments by O. Meyerhof (1912) which proved that when an organism is killed, no heat is given off. Thus, Pfeffer's formulations corresponded completely to the facts as they were finally known.[47,49]

b) Life without Oxygen

Already in 1878, Pfeffer made considerable experimental contributions to the understanding of the energy metabolism of organisms. In 1860, Louis Pasteur had shown that yeasts and certain bacteria could grow in the absence of oxygen.[48] Pasteur compared this ability with the already known fact that fruit in a room without oxygen will give off carbon dioxide and form alcohol. It took some years until this "life without oxygen" was generally accepted instead of other explanations (e.g., some oxygen is retained in the cells). Even outstanding scientists, such as Carl Nägeli, were convinced that life was fundamentally dependent on the presence of oxygen. To them, such actions as those described by Pasteur were physiological phenomena of no importance. In contrast, the animal physiologist Pflüger considered the reactions which persist after oxygen has been cut off as the direct cause of oxygen respiration. Between 1878 and 1889, Pfeffer carefully documented the similarities between respiration and fermentation as they relate to the substances involved, to certain genetic factors, and to the biological processes of energy metabolism. He explained in greater detail than Pasteur had done that the fruit and other organs of higher plants promptly form alcohol when oxygen is withheld. Pfeffer's investigations proved that the energy metabolism of bacteria and yeast is the same as the energy metabolism which takes place in oxygen respiration. He concluded that fermentation and respiration are similar processes as they relate to the energy exchange in the cell and to the biochemical steps in the break-down of sugar. To stress this similarity, he gave the name "intramolecular respiration" to the "respiration in the absence of oxygen." He also noted the "genetic link of the intramolecular respiration" with "fermentation and oxygen respiration."[48] Biochemical research in subsequent decades fully confirmed this concept. The production of alcohol during fermentation and the break-down of sugar (glycolysis) in oxygen respiration follow the same path for much of the way.

c) Energy Conversion of the Cell at Rest

Pfeffer was the first to have concrete ideas on how to interpret the energy conversion of the cell at rest. He believed that energy from chemical changes was involved only in visible or recognizable actions, such as in processes of secretion, in processes of concentration, and so on. He compared the condition of the cell at rest to that of a factory at rest. The "currents and transmissions" for the machinery continue to function, and this requires energy. The loss of heat by the organism at rest may be compared to the energy loss by friction of idling equipment in the factory after production has closed down. Pfeffer's comparison of the living cell with a leaking row-boat fits into this picture.

After Pfeffer, the first decisive advances in research on energy conversion in cells at rest was made by the Nobel Prize laureates Otto Warburg and Otto Meyerhof. They speculated that cells at rest would need energy to reverse the diffusion processes and chemical changes which normally proceed by themselves.[49] Today, it is known that the cell which is at rest and ready for action must have energy available. For example, energy is needed to maintain the membrane potential.

d) The Organism Does Not Have a Closed System of Energy

Pfeffer never had any doubts that the Second Law of thermodynamics was valid for living organisms. This was

75

disputed by biologists and philosophers even at a later date. They gave an incorrect interpretation for the apparent ability of living beings to operate in a contrary manner to an increase in entropy. This meant there was a progression from the "likely" to the "unlikely state" and perpetual motion was being realized. However, the organism does not possess a closed system of energy; Pfeffer recognized this, and all his writings show that he had no doubts in this matter. He specifically described "the totality of the event resulting from the activities inside and outside of the organism . . . as physiological performances" (1904, p.877). According to my interpretation [the author], he looked on life as a whirl within the changes in matter and in energy of the universe. The sub-title to his *Pflanzenphysiologie* is *Stoff-und Kraftwechsel in der Pflanze* [Metabolism and Changes in Energy in the Plant]. He could have continued the subtitle: A Whirl within the Changes in Matter and in Energy of the Universe. Pfeffer says, "Physiology, in particular, has as its final aim the investigation of the significance and the usage of the elemental means and forces supplied by the universe to living organisms for their building and their functioning. This should be Man's most difficult and most complex task on this planet."

Pfeffer stressed the close connection between changes in matter and changes in energy of the organism with those of the same changes in the universe as a whole. He also noted the close link between changes in matter and changes in energy. The separation of the two "is only due to practical considerations and a consequence of our mental attitudes which do not allow us to overcome the dualistic concept of matter and energy."[46] Following developments in modern physics, one could now add "at least not in our day."

12
ENDOGENOUS DIURNAL AND ANNUAL PERIODICITY

a) Circadian Leaf Movements

"Leaf Movements: Rosetta Stone of Plant Behavior?" This is the title of a paper by R.L. Satter and A.W. Galston published in 1973 in the field of plant physiology.[50] The title is very appropriate since the understanding of leaf movements is of such great significance to the understanding of plant physiology.

The diurnal rhythm of leaf movements was already recognized in the days of Alexander the Great. Androsthenes was on a campaign with Alexander when he observed these movements in some varieties of *Papilionaceae*. For the past 200 or more years there have been many reports on these kinds of movement. Major subjects for investigation were the opening and closing of flowers (studies of Linné), and the leaf movements of beans (fig. 13) and *Mimosa*. In the case of *Mimosa*, earlier workers, at times, confused the diurnal rhythms of the leaves with the movements caused by shaking; in both instances the movements follow the same course. The study of diurnal periodicity in leaf movements presented a host of problems, and to deal with them, Pfeffer undertook many experiments and introduced many technical innovations

Fig. 13 Primary leaves of beans (*Phaseolus*). These are the classic subjects of biological investigations on diurnal rhythms. The upward (daytime) and downward (nighttime) positions are guided by variations in turgor at the juncture of the leaf stalk and the leaf blade.

(cf. ch. 10). He devoted considerable thought to the subject, and he had to change his conclusions repeatedly. He began his investigations with the study of the opening and closing of petals. The results were published in *Physiologische Untersuchungen*, 1873, and this book was "dedicated in gratitude to my highly esteemed teachers, Herrn Professor, Dr. N. Pringsheim and Herrn Hofrat, Dr. J. Sachs." This was followed by the publication of a book in 1875 on *Periodische Bewegungen der Blattorgane* [periodical movements of leaf organs], "dedicated to Herrn Helmholtz with great admiration." The sequence in which the scientists are named mirrors Pfeffer's own development. Pringsheim had guided Pfeffer towards research in evolution, Sachs led him to plant physiology, and Helmholtz showed him the path to general physiology.

After 1875, Pfeffer did not undertake further research on diurnal periodicity until some thirty years later. Then between 1907 and 1915, he put out some 500 pages of publications on new experiments and findings.

The study of the diurnal movements of leaves and petals was Pfeffer's starting point for other fields of research: his osmotic investigations, his studies of the effect of temperature and light, and his studies of variations in turgor and in growth in connection with plant movements. It also had some bearing on a study of certain processes of regulation and of correlations between different leaves.

b) Hereditary or Conditioned Behaviour? The Darwin-Pfeffer Controversy

In the past, two problem areas presented great difficulties to biologists and even to scientists in other fields. In 1729, the French astronomer M. de Mairan noted that diurnal leaf movements could continue for some time in complete darkness, at a constant temperature. Thus, the plant seemed to know if it was day or night, even if it could not see the sun.[51] Until the start of the twentieth century, a controversy continued as to whether such behaviour could be due to an unknown external factor. The phenomenon also presented difficulties for Charles Darwin.[53] On the one hand, he was inclined to accept that the diurnal rhythm was a factor of heredity; on the other hand, he could not see any adaptive value in the leaf movements. They are not always simple upward and downward movements, such as the movements of beans. Complicated gyrations may be involved, including gyrations in which the leaf surface is completely folded together.

In 1880, Darwin wrote that anyone who observes the complexity of leaf movements cannot doubt that the movements have significance and thus an adaptive value (cf. fig. 14). However, nothing was discovered that proved this, and some twenty-five years later K. Semon concluded: "Since the endogenous diurnal movements do not have an adaptive value, this must be an imprint of a response to light and darkness which has become a hereditary imprint,

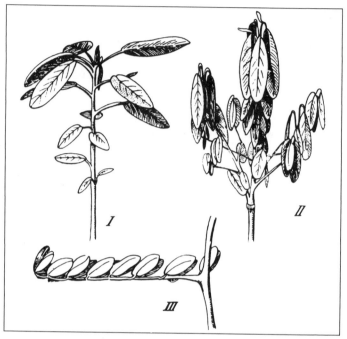

Fig. 14 *Desmodium gyrans*, in day position, I; in night position, II. *Coronilla rosea*, in night position, III. Copied from Darwin. Darwin states that the periodicity of the leaf movements have "to a certain extent" been inherited. The movements are sometimes so complex that the existence of an adaptive value must be assumed. — In contrast cf fig. 15 after Pfeffer.

that is to say, these are characteristics acquired through inheritance."[53] For disciples of Darwin, such as A. Weismann, these were serious arguments which they found difficult to accept.[53] Pfeffer too disagreed with Semon. In his early investigations on diurnal leaf movements, he had rejected the concept of a hereditary nature of the periodicity.

As an aside, it may be noted that Darwin voiced his opposition to Pfeffer's point of view in spite of the fact that he could not find an adaptive value to support his own opinion. He stated that he "could not follow Pfeffer's reasoning."

In those days, it was easy to think of external influences as the cause of movements. Jacques Loeb, the famous animal physiologist was teaching his theory of tropism. Loeb was a Professor of Physiology (of animals and humans) in Germany and later in the United States. From 1886 to 1888, he was a teaching assistant in Würzburg where he got to know Julius Sachs. He was intrigued by Sachs' studies on plant tropism — plant movements in response to stimuli. Loeb extended these findings to animals and to humans, eventually proposing that all behavior of plants, animals and humans was a connected series of tropisms. In a sense, he belongs to a group known as Behaviourists. Behaviourists believed (and still believe) that all reactions in psychology and in behavioural physiology are conditioned by external factors. However, this hypothesis has been disproved by zoologists who studied behavioural physiology. The names of the Nobel Prize laureates Nico Tinbergen and Konrad Lorenz come to mind. Lorenz is well known for his campaign against the behaviourists.[54]

Pfeffer — in the same manner as Loeb — started from the assumption that diurnal leaf movements were directly caused by changes in external conditions. The after-swings of leaf movements resembled the after-swings of a pendulum (fig. 15; also cf. quote p. 64). Thus Pfeffer continued to search for some other cause than the 24 hour light/dark rhythm as an explanation for the continued swings in darkness. He did not succeed in this although, on occasion, he thought he was on the right path. It must be remembered that at the time it was not known that a great

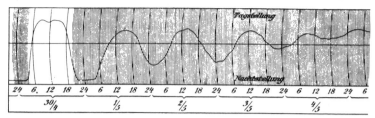

Fig. 15 The slowing down of the swings of bean leaves that have been kept in continuous darkness (shaded portion of figure). Copied from Pfeffer, 1907. On the basis of such results, Pfeffer concluded (1875 to 1907) that there is no inherited *Tagesautonomie*; there are only some after-swings "comparable to the swings of a pendulum." This was contrary to Darwin's idea. However, later, Pfeffer came to a different conclusion (cf. fig. 16, 1915).

amount of biological information is genetically stored and inherited. Today, there is quite a different perception, especially after the research done on animals by the Tinbergen and Lorenz schools. In Pfeffer's times, the notion that this would also be valid for plants was not even dreamt of. Today, we know that there is an "inner clock" (circadian rhythm) involved in the diurnal periodicity of leaf movements as well as in other physiological processes of plants and animals. These processes do have a high adaptive value.

As a result of research in aviation and space medicine, it is now known that a rhythm of activity can be imposed on animals and on humans which deviates from the 24 hour periodicity. For instance, a 10:10 or a 14:14 hour change in light/dark rhythm could be imposed; however, this would eventually lead to physiological problems. When the unusual rhythm is stopped, the subject promptly returns to the usual circadian periodicity without "after-swings." This characteristic is as valid for a single-celled organism as it is for Man, and this *Tagesautonomie* [endogenous diurnal behaviour] has a high adaptive value.

To say that all human behaviour can be shaped by conditioning is a serious fallacy in the opinion of K. Lorenz. Human behaviour cannot be changed or corrected in an unlimited way by conditioning.[54] It could be added that the same thing holds for plants, and Pfeffer acknowledged this in his later studies (1911, 1915). In doing this, he had to change his original erroneous opinion about the importance of conditioning. He developed experiments which clearly demonstrated the existence of a *Tagesautonomie*. The experiments show that oscillations last for many days when a single type of continuous light is applied. Moreover, the periods diverge from an exact 24 hour cycle (cf. fig. 16). Pfeffer showed clearly that the diurnal periodicity in the absence of the synchronizing light/dark cycle is only an approximate one (therefore the term "circadian" from *circa* "about" and *dies* "day").

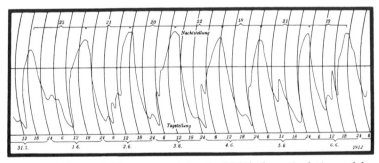

Fig. 16 Pfeffer, 1915: *Tagesautonomie* is a fact! With the articulations of the bean leaves wrapped in black cotton, the oscillations of the leaves carry on in continuous light (this part of the graph illustrates the swings in the second week after the last regular light-darkness cycle). The length of the periods no longer represent exact 24 hour cycles (in this case it may be seen that the periods are between 18 and 25 hours). Copied from Pfeffer, 1915.

Unfortunately, it was generally not known that Pfeffer, in his later years, undertook new research on diurnal periodicity. In consequence, the controversy on the subject was carried on unnecessarily for many years by experimenters who were much less skilled than Pfeffer. His work was overlooked outside of Germany because it was published during World War I. To make matters worse, his paper appeared in the journals of the *Königlich Sächsischen Gessellschaft der Wissenschaften* (Society of Sciences of the Kingdom of Saxony), not exactly a journal that would be readily available in the library of most departments of botany.

There remains no doubt that the diurnal periodicity of leaf movements must not be compared to the swings of a pendulum. However, it is understandable that such a comparison came readily to mind; all the more, since in plant tropism, return-swings and swings beyond the normal position are frequent after an irritation has occurred. Sometimes there is also a gradual slowing of swings before the normal position is resumed.

In 1792, F. v. P. Schrank already thought in terms of pendulum swings when he wrote about diurnal rhythms: "The movement does not end when the leaf has returned to the mid-point of its path where both opposite causes would be in balance; instead, it continues its movement in the starting direction until a counter force, which increases as the opposite force decreases, has won out."[55]

Such comparisons with the action of a pendulum may have led Pfeffer to investigate the effect of mechanical restrictions on the diurnal movements of leaves (1911). He discovered that a fundamental "impulse to motion" continues, even when the execution of the movements has been made impossible by mechanical means. Moreover, bending by coercive force did not have the reaction that could have been expected. After the leaves were again allowed to move freely, the phases of the swings returned to the same length as before the obstruction or coercive bending had been imposed.

c) The Self-regulatory Periodicity of Inherent Factors

Pfeffer had disproved his own earlier concepts with his latest experiments, and had demonstrated that the functioning of diurnal periodicity is not comparable to the wheels of a clock; rather, it is a peripheral function operated by an unknown clock. "In a self-regulatory manner a rhythmic change of inherent factors is brought about, and this results in the periodicity of movements or in the periodicity of other actions" (1915, p.137). Several years later, it was realized that this statement is equally valid for the sleep-wake rhythms of humans and animals; it is also valid for their daily rhythms of activity and rest. In 1922, C.P. Richter performed an experiment with rats which was analogous to Pfeffer's experiments with beans. Using electroshock, he rendered rats inactive for days. After the shock effects had worn off, the rats resumed their activities according to their normal rhythm as if nothing had happened. Furthermore, there was no shift in the phases of the rhythms.[56]

Once Pfeffer had published the conclusions of his experiments in 1915, the diurnal periodicity of leaf movements should no longer have been regarded as an isolated phenomenon of the physiology of movement. In fact, in 1897 he had already stated that there were phenomena of diurnal periodicity which possibly "were the result of other sources of periodic activities in the plant." In this case as in other cases, it took decades before the connection to Pfeffer's work was taken up again.

After his discovery of new facts about diurnal periodicity, Pfeffer was forced to revise most of his concepts of the past thirty-five to forty years. His far-ranging discussions of his findings with all the pros and cons illustrates the extent to which physiologists were puzzled by the newly discovered phenomena.

d) Advances and Reversals after Pfeffer

The subject that Pfeffer once called *Tagesautonomie* has today become a major area of research. Many biological and medical research institutions are investigating *Tagesautonomie* as it relates to day and night rhythms, to sleep and wakefulness, to rapid flight, to shift work, et cetera. In all of this research, plants and single-celled organisms are widely used.[57]

Pfeffer's investigations of endogenous diurnal periodicity were performed with great care and skill, and they led to many far-reaching conclusions. It is difficult to understand how other authors after Pfeffer published such second-rate reports on the same subject. Many vague hypotheses were proposed about unknown external factors, in spite of the fact that they had long ago been disproved by Pfeffer. Of course, as has been pointed out, his work was unfortunately published in a journal that was not widely circulated. One can only marvel at how he conceived the ideas for his advanced experiments when it took other workers decades to understand the very basis of the ideas. In 1928, A. Kleinhoonte was finally able to set up satisfactory experiments resulting in good curves — comparable to those of Pfeffer's — for the diurnal leaf movements of *Canavalia*. Kleinhoonte also referred in detail to Pfeffer's work.[58]

In recent times, many subjects related to diurnal periodicity have been presented as new discoveries;

however, they had been dealt with by Pfeffer long ago. For instance, there is the desynchronization within a single plant (i.e., individual leaves of a plant follow their own rhythms with differing phase lengths). Another example is the use of an imposed synchronization on the usual rhythm. Thus, a normal rhythm of approximately 24 hours may be synchronized to follow a rhythm of an exact 24 hour cycle by imposing an external cycle of 12:12 hours of alternating light and darkness. Higher frequencies, such as 6:6 and 2:2 hours of light and darkness cycles, can also be used for synchronization.

e)   Self-Regulation of Annual Periodicity

The discovery of the *Tagesautonomie* meant that Pfeffer had to revise his older concepts; but this did not shatter his *Weltbild* [philosophy of life]. He had never believed in a behaviourist dogma in which all types of reaction were the result of outside conditioning. At an early date, a careful analysis of all available data had led him to recognize the existence of an inherited annual periodicity. Today, it has been proven that the annual periodicity of developmental cycles and behavioural cycles of animals and plants can be made to continue under constant artificial conditions in the laboratory. Here again, it has been found that there is not an exact agreement with the external periodicity, and for that reason the term "circannual periodicity" is used. Zoologists have believed that the discovery of the circannual periodicity is of recent date, and more specifically, that it was first found in birds. It was forgotten that Pfeffer had recommended that plant and animal physiology should be dealt with as one in research on annual periodicity (1893). Pfeffer tended to favour the thesis of conditioning, that is to say the influence of external rhythms with some after-swings; nevertheless, he also concluded that there was an "autogenous [self-engendered] annual periodicity" which was "the result of an inherited rhythmics acting together with the after-effect of the rhythmics." He spoke of the "creative supremacy of self-regulation" (1904).

13

CORRELATIONS: THE STUDY OF "IRRELEVANT DETAILS" WITH UNEXPECTED CONSEQUENCES

In 1921, Karl von Goebel, the great botanist and expert in morphology wrote, "It is alarming to see how stimulus physiologists are obstinate in studying completely irrelevant details." There is no doubt that in all fields of biological research, needless time has often been spent on details. If no new ideas are generated, such research may easily deteriorate to the level of an amateur's collection of butterflies or stamps. The examination of details is only of value if it serves as a lever to penetrate deeper into universal laws. It is evident that Pfeffer used details as such a lever or "tool" (cf.p. 20). Pfeffer's studies of the stamens of varieties of *Centraurea* led him to his investigation of osmosis. The successful results of his study of endogenous diurnal variations is another example of his use of detail. A further example relates to Pfeffer's interest in the significant role of correlations. He says:

> All functions of life consist of chains of interactions; the varied and universally correlating influence of all parts is absolutely necessary in the face of all outside changes in order to create and maintain the conditions for growth and existence. In view of such close

> interdependency, an autonomous or induced change in one organ must be reflected in the remaining organs, even though such change may often be imperceptible. In matter of fact, every chapter of physiology offers proof of the conspicuous interaction between parts of a plant organism (1897, p. 22).

Darwin had already come across such a correlation.[52] He introduced the use of grass shoots or, more precisely, the use of their coleoptile as subjects for the study of phototropism — the bending of a plant in response to light (cf.fig.17). He found that the locus for the reception of the stimulus is separate from the location of the reaction. The stimulus is received at the tip of the coleoptile. The bending occurs much lower down as the side facing the light grows differentially to the side away from the light. There has to be, therefore, a "stimulus transmission."[60]

It did not take long before Darwin's conclusions were vigorously attacked. At Pfeffer's suggestion, Rotherd took up the question again in 1894. Darwin's results were confirmed, and they were further refined. It was found that, even after the vascular tissues were severed, the "stimulus" was transmitted to the lower, reactive zone. In spite of this, it was still assumed that the "stimulus transmission" took place through living cells outside of the vascular tissue. At first, this was also Pfeffer's opinion. However, Peter Boysen Jensen in Copenhagen had performed experiments that pointed in a different direction. He continued his experiments in Pfeffer's laboratory, and was able to prove that living cells are not needed for the "stimulus transmission." Boysen Jensen relates, "at first the *Geheimrat* was skeptical, rejecting; gradually he started to waver. In the end, he was convinced, and he said, 'this is really of eminent significance!' " These investigations were continued by Boysen Jensen, now back in Copenhagen, and by Paál

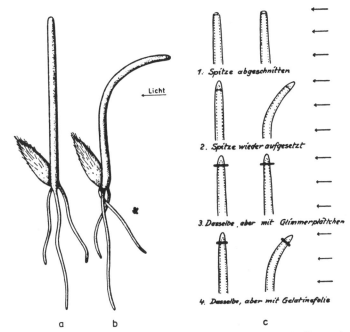

Licht

1. *Spitze abgeschnitten*

2. *Spitze wieder aufgesetzt*

3. *Dasselbe, aber mit Glimmerplättchen*

4. *Dasselbe, aber mit Gelatinefolie*

a   b   c

Fig. 17 Oat seedling with the coleoptile growing vertically or bent phototropically in response to light from the side.

Darwin: The tip receives the stimulus. Without the tip the coleoptile (cl) can no longer respond. The reaction zone lies considerably lower.

Research in Pfeffer's laboratory: The "stimulus transmission" is based on a substance which is able to diffuse across the cut section (c2), and even through a sheet of gelatine (c4). A thin plate of mica prevents the "stimulus transmission" (c3).

Follow-up: Extensive research of growth substances, manufacture of synthetics, application in agriculture and horticulture.

(a) and (b) copied from Mohr, *Pflanzenphysiologie*, 2nd ed. (Heidelberg: Springer Verlag, 1971). (c)copied from Walter, fig.5.

91

(from Budapest) who was working in Pfeffer's laboratory. The findings show that the "stimulus transmission" can occur even when the locus of the reception of the stimulus and the location of the reaction are separated experimentally from each other. The severed tip may be illuminated alone; if it is then put back on the basel portion of the shoot, bending occurs. Bending can also be induced, if the coleoptile receives a cut instead of being illuminated. Paál (1914) had this to say: "In this case of bending, the incision neutralizes the normal correlating effect which would be transmitted evenly from the tip to the growth zone. The carriers of these growth regulating effects, as in the case of phototropic stimulus transmission, are as yet unidentified substances which can diffuse through gelatine."

After these investigations, the oat coleoptiles continued to be a significant tool in investigations of the physiology of growth and motion. Von Goebel, the famous researcher who was mentioned above, wrote in 1927, "Papers on morphology are no longer read or used for reference. The coleoptile of *Avena sativa* seems to be the only subject of serious scientific research. Yet, in my opinion, very little of significance results! Morphology is, after all, the most important characteristic of organisms."[63] These sentences characterize the attitude faced by the budding field of plant physiology. Physiologists were not deterred. The investigations of F.W. Went of Utrecht were another large step forward.[64] They were published shortly after von Goebel's criticism, and they were closely tied to the research methods of Boysen Jensen and Paál.

He placed the cut-off coleoptile tips (again, of oats) on blocks of agar, and the yet unknown substance was absorbed. When the blocks were then placed on tip-less coleoptile stumps, bending resulted. From the rate of diffusion of the substance, he gained the first clues about the size of the molecules of the yet unknown "auxins."

These and other growth substances are now well known. The Avena-test (Oat = *Avena sativa*) is still being used. Synthetically produced growth substances are now widely used in horticulture and in agriculture to facilitate the rooting of cuttings, to produce seedless fruits, to fight broad-leafed (di-cotyledonal) varieties of weeds on lawns and in grain fields, to control the dormancy period of potatoes, and so on.[65]

Something did result after all. As Pfeffer said (cf. above) it was of "eminent significance."

14
FLAWS IN LITERARY STYLE

The following sentence appears in Wöhler's evaluation of Pfeffer's doctoral thesis: "With regard to style, there are many flaws." While the faculty disregarded these flaws, they should not be simply attributed to the missing years of high school education. It is still an effort to work through Pfeffer's later publications. His latest work on the periodicity of leaf movements consisted of 150 pages. Today, the standards of most scientific journals would require that this should be compressed to about twenty pages. Almost every sentence in Pfeffer's works reflects the complexity of biological phenomena and the resulting complexity of arguments and counter-arguments, as well as the to and fro of the deliberations of the experimenter and the writer. Everywhere, questions are raised, and reservations and qualifications are made. Pfeffer's publications, including his *Handbuch der Pflanzenphysiologie*, are a continuation of the many discussions which he held regularly with his students and with his co-workers. He could never bring himself to simplify and thereby risk inaccuracies for the sake of accommodating beginners. Anybody who has taught biology in school or at university knows that in this science — more than in physics and chemistry — the beginner benefits only when simplified explanations are given, even though these explanations may not be entirely or universally valid. This is especially the case if biology is not presented as a collection of isolated facts, but is taught as a field of science. It should be shown how facts relate to other facts and to unresolved problems, and indeed, how they are linked with the entire theoretical and experimental structure of natural science. One example may serve to show how Pfeffer expressed himself. In his investigations of leaf movements, published in 1875, he writes about a topic which today could be seen as unrelated to the main subject:

> The observation of immobility during darkness points inevitably to internal cell processes about which we are still ignorant. We can hardly hope to get some insight by direct observation, but instead, we should look for a suitable combination of phenomena which bears a relationship to individual functions. To avoid such experiments means to give up hope of ever lifting the veil which hides the life of cells. This could hardly be the intent of any investigator who does not see organic life as emanating from any other forces than those which control the inorganic substances of our planet and of all heavenly bodies, no matter, that these forces may be only incompletely known, or may as yet be undiscovered. However, we must at all times be fully aware that the attempt to penetrate the inner workings of the cell and the complex relationships of its functions is only the tentative beginning of a hypothesis.

Pfeffer's familiar quotation, often heard in his laboratory, was, *"es kann sein, es muss aber nicht sein"* [it may be, but is not necessarily so;] it was characteristic of his manner of expressing himself in speech and in writing. My own copy [Bünning] of Pfeffer's *Handbuch* comes from the estate of the famous botanist, Karl von Goebel. There are quite a number of marginal notes by von Goebel regarding the style of writing, as for instance, "Oh Lord, is this really German?" Pfeffer's works continued to be a rich source of information, but as Gottlieb Haberlandt wrote in 1915, " . . . in view of the obviously cumbersome style, only a very slow study with frequent retracing can be of lasting benefit to the reader. There are probably only a few scientific works which force the reader to participate in a productive, mental effort to the same extent, as is the case with Pfeffer's *Pflanzenphysiologie*."[1]

Pfeffer's "flaws in literary style" are largely the result of his choosing not to offer easy definitions, as was done, for instance, by the frequently cited Jacques Loeb. To Loeb most things were very simple and clear.[8]

15
PURKINJE - J. MÜLLER -
HELMHOLTZ - SACHS - PFEFFER

In 1840, Purkinje opened one of the first German institutes for physiology in Breslau. Before that, he had been conducting experiments in his own home. Purkinje did not pursue individual problems in a consequential manner; however, he was a successful observer and experimenter in several areas of anatomy and physiology, and he showed great ingenuity in the development of equipment. He and Johannes Müller are considered to be the founders of experimental physiology in Germany. The path from Purkinje leads via Sachs to Pfeffer. The young Julius Sachs used to play with Purkinje's children in the garden of Purkinje's house in Breslau, and he was greatly influenced by the elder Purkinje. After Sachs became an orphan at the age of seventeen, he worked as a laboratory helper for Purkinje in Prague. The stimulus he received in doing experiments stood him well when he eventually founded modern plant physiology.[66] It is worth noting that many outstanding research scientists did not simply continue in the same field and in the same manner as their teachers; instead, they transferred what they had learned to other fields, and continued their own research along completely new paths. Sachs switched from using animals and humans in experimental physiology to the investigation of plants. At the same time, however, his methods of investigation followed those of Purkinje. Many of Sachs' students continued in the field pioneered by him; they worked in plant physiology, a field of botany which had been neglected until then.

Pfeffer went beyond Sachs. He saw plant physiology as a way to advance the general laws of biology. In 1893, in addressing a meeting of the Association of German Naturalists and Physicians, he said:

> It is of greatest importance for physiological research to consider plants and animals at the same time. All knowledge of natural science is based on comparative observations, and one of the most important tools to penetrate ever deeper, and to separate the significant from the insignificant is the broadening of our horizon to encompass as great a variety of phenomena as possible. For this reason, it is very important and necessary that our knowledge of animal and vegetable matter be referred to when dealing with general questions. Animal physiology should be able to benefit from plant physiology, just as plant physiology benefits from its sister science. Without being presumptuous, plant physiology can pride itself for having broadened our horizon in the last decades through purposeful research, and for having given us a clear or improved understanding of many life processes.

Sachs, and many of Pfeffer's contemporaries did not grasp the significance of these and other demands voiced by Pfeffer. Also, Sachs had no appreciation of the osmotic investigations performed by his "students," Pfeffer and de Vries. He found Pfeffer's osmotic experiments barely worthy of a short notation. Even Pfeffer's students, and also contemporary and later botanists, thought it possible to evaluate Sachs and Pfeffer in relation to each other. In this connection, statements by Fitting are of interest. To him we owe an excellent and comprehensive presentation of Pfeffer's life and achievements. He made the following evaluation:

> Sachs was without a doubt more passionate; he was consumed by his work. Pfeffer, on the other hand, was cool and careful, thinking ahead methodically in the conduct of his life, and husbanding the strength of his not too robust body. This difference in personality also characterizes their achievements. Sachs was more daring. He did not hesitate to use his phantasy and to express exciting, new ideas, and he pushed for their acceptance even when it was obvious to critical observers that they were biased or limited — he was a fighter. On the other hand, Pfeffer, serious and cautious, was rather anxiously reserved, and he tended to secure his position on all sides. He was concerned about making a mistake in his lectures or in his scientific writings. He used to say that he did not want to make a fool of himself. Sachs was the more versatile one, who with his burning intellect was able to embrace the whole body of general botany, who would thoughtfully present its history, and who wrote a leading textbook of the entire field of botany, a textbook which was a standard for many years. He was the more brilliant, seductive spirit with an artistic, intuitive talent and a thorough education in philosophy. He was a captivating master of elocution and of literary presentation. He was able to evoke enthusiasm for botany, even among those who were outside the field. In contrast, Pfeffer's mastery revealed itself in the wise restraint which he consciously imposed upon himself and in his ability to think profoundly. As a result of his specialization, he tended to show less esteem for the other fields of botany.[1]

These are striking characterizations by one of Pfeffer's most successful co-workers. However, these characterizations do not seem complete, unless one adds that Pfeffer did not see himself as a botanist in the traditional sense, or as a plant physiologist in the sense of Sachs. He saw himself as a general physiologist. Sachs supplied him with the "tool" — plant physiology. Hermann von Helmholtz was his model for setting a goal. Helmholtz could rightly be called a physiologist and a physicist. He was one of the discoverers of the law of the conservation of energy along with the physician, Julius Robert Mayer, and the physicist, James Prescott Joule. For good reason, Pfeffer dedicated one of his early publications to Helmholtz (cf.p. 78).

Sachs did not really understand the idea of relating physiological processes to universal laws. He is even said to have called Pfeffer's *Pflanzenphysiologie* a "heap of undigested facts." He writes that, regretfully, Pfeffer "has gotten himself into a purely physical mess."[66] What Pfeffer intended is already expressed in the subtitle of his *Handbuch der Pflanzenphysiology* — "A Treatise upon the Metabolism and Sources of Energy in Plants." The morphology was certainly not his aim. Many did not understand his intentions, and therefore, they even ridiculed the subtitle.[67]

The scientific forerunner of von Helmholtz, the physician and physiologist J. Müller, had formulated the precept of the specific energies of the senses. Irrespective of what causes a sensory organ, such as the eye, to be stimulated — be it light, an impact, or electricity — the stimulus transmitted by nerve impulses leads always to the same "sensations." In the case of the eyes, this is always a light sensation (today, one no longer speaks of specific "energies" in this case). Although he constantly emphasized the common relationship of all organisms, Pfeffer immediately recognized that the law of specific energies could not be applied to plants. Sachs had tried to do this. Pfeffer strongly rejected such a transferability (1893d). He said:

> A plant, or even an individual organ of a plant, is never sensitive to only one type of stimulus; and therefore, heterogeneous processes of stimulation can occur simultaneously . . . . This proves, furthermore, that any stimulus in a plant, or in a single cell does not produce the same result. The cell does not act like our eye in which different kinds of irritations produce a sensation of light. Such a selective ability of an organ — specific energies in the sense of Johannes Müller is out of the question in plants.

Pfeffer had recognized that in the case of lower organisms, all abilities exist within the organism, or even within the single cell of a unicellular organism (cf.p. 45). A marked specialization of individual organs to fulfill distinct sensory functions occurs only in higher organisms with morphological differentiations.

More could be said regarding Pfeffer's "low regard" for other fields of botany. Having quoted von Goebel's remarks (cf.p. 92), it may be added that the disapproval was a mutual one. But something else lies behind this. The development of each branch of biology is characterized by pioneers who open new fields. However, some successors frequently get lost in the search for additional examples or details, and their work becomes insignificant. Without a doubt, some of Pfeffer's epigones fit into this category. Only a select number were of the stature of a Carl Correns or a Keita Shibata (cf.p. 106). (It is no coincidence that the Correns couple were among the closer friends of the Pfeffer household.)[75]

16
THE SPREAD OF "PFEFFERGEWÄCHSE" [PEPPER PLANTS] THROUGHOUT THE WORLD

a) Pfeffer's 265 Students

Pfeffer's fame and success and the work of his students led to a decreased interest in plant morphology. As could be expected, many botanists resented this. Von Goebel wrote, "As of late, faculties do not want any part of the *Piperaceas* (pepper plants) and their one-sided outlook. Even so, they will all get ahead; a large number of professorships in botany must be filled."[68] However, not every morphologist was a von Goebel, and on the whole, the career successes of the *Piperaceas* greatly advanced the study of modern biology. In Germany, systematic botany missed making a connection with genetics. By the time the "new systematics" blossomed in America, it was already too late. Even the morphologists and anatomists — except for men like von Goebel and Haberlandt — got side-tracked to details of less and less significance. There always seemed to be another species whose vascular tissue could be studied for a doctoral thesis.

Pfeffer had numerous students. There were some 265 in all, which included post-graduate students. Nearly half of this number were to become university professors in Germany and in other countries. His co-workers came from all "civilized countries" (as they were then called) of the old and of the new world. Many in particular, came from the United States, from Imperial Russia, and from the Scandinavian countries. Professor B. M. Duggar of the Missouri Botanical Garden wrote, "No German professor has done more than Professor Pfeffer to promote botanical work in this country [the USA]".[69]

A number of Pfeffer's students and co-workers became very important botanists, and their achievements are still widely quoted. Many of them actually founded plant physiology in their home countries. Even today, numerous biologists in German-speaking countries and in several other countries regard Pfeffer as their mentor.

No less a figure than Carl Correns had this to say: "The effort and care which he directed toward their training was quite unusual. He was always ready to help, and he was constantly willing to show his students how to overcome their difficulties. Above all, there was his penetrating and wholesome critique of their results. In this way, he influenced even those students who later followed quite different paths than his own."[70]

To describe the achievements of these collaborators would be to write a part of the history of plant physiology from Pfeffer to the present time. One example is Keita Shibata of Tokyo. In 1910, at the age of thirty-three, Shibata resigned from his post as professor with the Faculty of Agriculture of the University of Sapporo in order to study plant physiology with Pfeffer in Leipzig, and also to study organic chemistry with M. Freud in Frankfurt. Subsequently, Shibata exerted a major influence in his own country. He played a leading role in the rapid development of research both in plant biochemistry, and in microbiology oriented towards chemistry. He founded the internationally recognized journal, *Acta Phytochimica.* The impact of the impressions Shibata gained in Germany is evidenced by the fact that he wrote all the drafts for his lectures in German. All scientific expressions which he taught his Japanese students were in German. At first, he accepted only papers written in German for publication in *Acta Phytochimica.*

Articles written in memory of Shibata[71] show the influence of Pfeffer and the parallels to Pfeffer: "He first visited Professor W. Pfeffer in Leipzig and under the guidance of this world-famous scholar he studied the 'loose combination of oxygen by some colour producing bacteria' . . . . Many active biochemists and plant physiologists sprouted from under his arm just as seedlings of a great tree dispersed beneath its wide spread branches" (Hattori). Hiroshi Tamiya, who also studied under Shibata writes in a later memorial address for his teacher: "It is not an exaggeration to say that alone the chronological list of Shibata's works represents a history of the development of Japanese botany since the flourishing of Western sciences in Japan." Shibata started with systematic, morphological and anatomical works. There followed investigations of the chemotaxis of spermatozoids of ferns. Next, there was a transition to various sub-branches of biochemistry. For instance, there is a book (1936) about the catalytic effects of metallic compounds. His course of development is very similar to Pfeffer's (cf.p. 18). There is another parallel: The laboratory where Pfeffer worked with such success was destroyed by bombing in the Second World War; Shibata's home was also destroyed by bombs.

This is only one example, among many, of Pfeffer's influence and of the wide-ranging influence of scientists of stature of that time. It also shows how much we [Germans] have gambled away what others had built up with great effort.

No doubt, some of Pfeffer's students obtained an academic chair more on the basis of having worked with him than on the basis of outstanding qualifications. However, this does not detract from the massive impetus which was given to botany by Pfeffer and his students. In contrast, progress in zoology (in Germany) was held back by the emphasis on morphology.

b) The High Repute of Botany in Germany at the Turn of the Century

Few biologists realize the extent of the world's esteem for German botany around the turn of the century. Unfortunately, much of this esteem was subsequently gambled away as a result of wars and political events.

What E. Strasburger wrote in 1898 is absolutely to the point:

> Most of the outstanding botanists to whom Germany owes its lead in botany are dead. The development of botanical science in this century will indisputably remain associated with the names of Carl Nägeli, Hugo von Mohl, Wilhelm Hofmeister, Julius Sachs, Anton de Bary, Nathan Pringsheim, and to a lesser degree Alexander Braun. The numerous foreigners who still come to Germany every year to obtain their "Ordination" as botanists tend to go to Wilhelm Pfeffer in Leipzig, or they come here to Bonn.

In those days, it was a special honour for a non-German botanist to be made a member of the German Botanical Society. In his book on Eduard Strasburger (1967), B. Holzmann writes: "Thus, Strasburger was asked by F.A.F.C. Went (The Hague, May16, 1889), and by Bradley Moore Davies (Chicago, June 20, 1898) to recommend them for membership. For the same purpose, Charles Joseph

Chamberlain of the Department of Botany, University of Chicago, interceded for a young Japanese scientist, '. . . It would give me great pleasure, if you would propose Dr. Shigeo Yamanouchi for membership in the German Botanical Society. I know he would consider it an even greater honour if you were the one to suggest or propose his name for candidate . . .' (January 23, 1908).''[72]

17

WHERE DID THE GREAT SPIRIT ORIGINATE? HIS CHARACTER

a) The Ancestors

Pfeffer's contemporaries felt that they could not measure up to him. Even Haberlandt, as outstanding a figure as he was, wrote that he did not feel at ease in Pfeffer's presence. "Later I saw him repeatedly, but in the presence of this genius and this very critical scientist, I always felt intimidated as if exposed to a blast of ice-cold wind."[73]

In the case of personalities such as Pfeffer, there arises the question of heritage, both from the point of view of biological descent and of family tradition. There were pharmacists, clergymen and "scribes" among Pfeffer's ancestors. This was typical of the family background of many of the famous men of that period. Yet this explanation seems inadequate to understand a great spirit such as Pfeffer.

Zionists, including H. R. Oppenheimer, claimed that Pfeffer belonged to that group of Jews who had renounced their faith. Oppenheimer spoke of the great impetus that was given botany when the medieval ghettos were opened. Oppenheimer writes "and European enlightenment was allowed to spread among the Jews. This phenomenon may be considered as analogous with the rise

111

of humanism in the Christian world. The personality of W. Pfeffer for instance, may only be understood by reference to the discipline in logic bequeathed by many generations of Jewish education combined with the freedom of thought granted the individual by an era of liberalism."[74]

As appropriate as these considerations may be, a Jewish descent for Pfeffer cannot be established. There is a great-grandparent on the father's side (Samuel Weiss) who may have been Jewish, but there is no proof. Pfeffer's wife knew nothing of a tradition of Jewish descent. She was angry at Oppenheimer's claim, and she called it a distortion of the truth. On the other hand, Pfeffer's daughter-in-law, who despised the Nazis, said, "wonderful!"

Pfeffer's appearance and his sharp logic were attributed by the family to his French heritage on his mother's side.[75] His mother's grandfather was pastor of the French Huguenot community in Hanau.

Stippel, in his recollections (cf.p. 15) makes comments which support the marked genetic influence of the mother. "She was a stately, beautiful woman . . . with full cheeks, a slightly curved nose, and dark brown hair. Her son, Willi, seems to have inherited the latter from her, and also his general facial features . . . he had little resemblance to his father."

This is all we know, and in fact, all we probably need to know about this question, even though it has often been asked.

b) Character Traits

Heritage and environment, including traditional family values combined providentially to form Pfeffer's personality. This holds true, not only for the acuteness of his thinking, but also for the character traits which played a significant role in his success. For the description of these characteristics, one has to rely on the reports of contemporaries and of family members. It is not unusual to speak only good of the dead. However, reports are so definite and so unanimous regarding Pfeffer's personality that one need not hesitate to accept them as factual. The character traits which are emphasized again and again are kindliness, fairness, conscientiousness, thoroughness and a sense of duty.

Many colleagues were somewhat afraid of his critical mind. Yet, it is unanimously reported that Pfeffer, while he was revered and while he inspired respect — as an old man he was even patriarchal — he was always simple, natural, friendly and kind. In dealing with others, he was just as circumspect and measured as in his scientific discussions. He did not like public prominence, nor did he aspire to high office.

Order, punctuality, and exactness were as important in his personal life as in his scientific work. There still exists the draft of a letter which he wrote on September 28, 1918 when he was searching for his son who had been reported "missing in action." (His son had in fact been killed on September 1, 1918.) It is apparent that every word was checked, small changes made, words added, words erased before the final letter was written. It was fortuitous that the draft of this letter was discovered. Pfeffer's dislike of matters that had not been thought out, and of matters for which the outcome had not been fully evaluated led him to destroy many papers shortly before his death. Letters and documents were systematically destroyed; unfortunately, these included completed records of two major research projects. He did not have the strength or concentration to transcribe them, nor did he wish them to fall unfinished into other hands. His conscientious management of all matters, large or small, shows up in his last letters to his daughter-in-law; he discusses matters of money and property in detail.

Pfeffer's character traits contributed to the deterioration of his health. In a Germany which was starved by the Allied blockade, he refused to eat more than the small ration to which he was entitled.

18
DUTIES WITHIN THE UNIVERSITY

a) General

Many great scientists succeeded by isolating themselves in their laboratory and by letting others take care of teaching and administrative duties. Pfeffer attended to all these duties in a most conscientious manner. At his funeral service, the representative for the faculty had this to say:

> Pfeffer's great spirit, his clear intellect, his critical sense, all worked to the benefit of the scientific community to which he belonged — the University and the closer circle of the Faculty of Philosophy. Just as he devoted his life to scientific work, he devoted much effort in the service of the community. In meetings, his clear, precise judgment was often decisive in settling difficult questions. His critical caution frequently avoided overly rash decisions.

There still exist numerous memoranda and letters which testify to Pfeffer's endeavours to improve the facilities for teaching. In a twelve page submission to his faculty at the University of Tübingen, dated October 14, 1878, he pointed to the need of offering experience in laboratory work to students in botany and to students who were taking botany as a secondary subject. In those days, few institutions had botanical laboratories. The submission was accompanied

Fig. 18 The Institute of Botany in Leipzig where Pfeffer worked from 1887 to 1920. It was destroyed by bombs in the Second World War.

by building sketches which show that he had given careful thought to structural alterations at the institute.

Pfeffer refused to accept any position that went beyond the many responsibilities of a full professorship. For that reason, he declined the post of Rector of the University of Leipzig, a highly esteemed position, but one that was mainly representative.

b) Hermann Ullrich: Reminiscences on Studies with Pfeffer (A Personal Report)

In early December 1918, a large number of servicemen were demobilized, and I was one of many who were in a hurry to study at a university. The winter semester was already in progress, and we arrived in the middle of the lectures and the lab work. I wanted to take biology as my major, and among other courses I registered for "Experimental Physiology of Plants" and for "Beginners' Experiments Using A Microscope." The calendar of the University of Leipzig, from which I chose the courses, indicated that they would be given by Dr. Pfeffer.

I expected to be able to follow the lectures, but handling the laboratory experiments for first year students was a different matter. I was only able to manage because I had owned a microscope in my school years, and I had already acquired some experience with its use. The course was overcrowded with eighty to ninety participants, but there were only forty work spaces available. Thus, the course had to be given in two sessions. Normally, it was given Tuesdays and Fridays from 10 a.m. to 12 noon. I do not remember at which point I had joined the program; however, I vividly remember how *Geheimrat* Pfeffer — a slightly stooped man — spoke to me reassuringly the first time he came to my work space. I was immediately freed of my nervousness as a beginner.

Full of expectation, I went to my first lecture given by Pfeffer; it was the first lecture I had ever attended. After some effort, I found a seat in the back of the lecture hall — a hall shaped like an amphitheatre. Pfeffer paced slowly back and forth behind his long lecture table while speaking in a rather low voice. From the back rows, it was difficult to follow what he said. One thing, though, struck me immediately — the extremely careful formulation of his statements. It was the first time that I heard him say, *"es kann so sein, es bräucht aber nit so zu sein"* [it may be, but is not necessarily so]. It was a rhetorical phrase which he often used and which will remain fixed in my memory, as it probably is in the memory of all of Pfeffer's students. I was able to follow the lectures reasonably well once I had looked into some of the available literature, and I had prepared myself for the coming lessons. Pfeffer's lectures in

117

experimental plant physiology were quite demand-
ing, and for beginners they were especially difficult.
For that reason, we took the lecture series over again
in the following winter semester.

Pfeffer was very popular as an examiner, especially
when it was for state examinations. In spite of his high
standards, he was able to dispel the jitters of the
candidates. When a candidate could not answer a
question at the examination — they were held in
public — Pfeffer would soothingly say, "Well now,
let's leave that."

According to the university calendar, Pfeffer was to
give a daily lecture on general botany from 7 to 8 a.m.
However, as a result of the large influx of returning
war veterans, Pfeffer was forced to give his lectures
twice, and he did this daily from 6 to 7 a.m. The lecture
hall was meant to accommodate 200; by adding chairs
and benches, the capacity was increased to 260. Yet,
some four to five hundred wanted to attend the
lecture, and even with many standing, there still was
insufficient space. Before each lecture, Pfeffer had a
plant placed at every desk. He would first talk about
this plant from the point of view of morphology,
ecology and systematics. When I was there, he started
with a *Ranunculacea*, I believe it was *Ficaria verna*, and he
continued his systematic discussion from *Rosaceae* to
Symnpetaleae. Then he switched — often quite abruptly
— to the main topic of his lecture. He started his
comprehensive lecture for beginners with a discussion of the place of biology in natural sciences. He
considered life as a process which is tied to biological
structures through a continuous exchange in energy
and matter. This was central to his point of view as a
physiologist. The course then covered questions of
growth, the basics of systematics, cell physiology, and
the general physiology of metabolism. The latter dealt
with such questions as respiration, photosynthesis
and other processes of assimilation. Even today, very
little has changed in this arrangement of lectures.

Pfeffer's explanations were rather matter-of-fact, almost dry, very carefully formulated and long-winded. The attentive student who followed his train of thought was left with the perception that the science of botany still had many unanswered questions. It was not easy to take notes, and afterwards, they had to be thoroughly worked over.

For those students who had lost time because of war service, the University of Leipzig had a special semester from February to April 1919, a period which was normally a vacation. During this period, Pfeffer gave a lecture on basic botany from 11 a.m. to 12 noon on Monday, Tuesday, Thursday and Friday. On Wednesday and Saturday, from 11 a.m.to 1 p.m., he spent his time with first year students who were doing experiments that required the use of the microscope.

I have many more recollections of the second time I attended the course on Experimental Plant Physiology in the winter semester 1919-20. Pfeffer followed the usual procedure of having the teaching assistant set up the materials for many demonstrations and experiments. Frequently, the set-ups would relate to the subject of the previous lecture, especially if the preparation required much time and effort. Pfeffer would use this for a short review. He would then use other experiments to illustrate his presentation — a presentation which had always been carefully thought out. If an experiment did not work out the first time, he could barely conceal his dissatisfaction. As an example, there was the occasion when the continued growth of a primary leaf of grain immersed in a drop of water under the microscope was to be projected on to the screen (arc lights were still in use). However, the water drop kept running off the slide, and the tip of the leaf did not appear in the projection. The experiment only succeeded after Pfeffer — always a skillful experimenter — took over; he checked all adjustments with a steady hand, and then successfully placed the immersion droplet on the slide under the microscope.

In the winter semester of 1919-20, we saw the microscopic projections which Pfeffer had already described in the year 1900; the protoplasmic streaming, the plasmolysis, and the formation and growth of precipitation membranes. Examples of projections in silhouette were the stimulation of tendrils, the thermonastic opening of tulip buds, and the formation of oxygen bubbles — very impressive — with *Elodea*. In the latter case, it was demonstrated that the magnitude of the stream of bubbles depended on the light intensity (a diffuse light was obtained by using a wire mesh). Pfeffer also presented time-lapse photos of the following subjects: the geotropic raising to an upright position of a plant of *Impatiens glandulifera*, the sleep movements of *Desmodium gyrans*, the movements of *Mimosa spegazzinii*, and the germination of *Vicia faba*. He also demonstrated the nutation of the pedicel, and the blossoming and withering of tulips.

There was an abundance of material being presented on the demonstration bench. Experiments after Engelmann showed the concentration of aerobic bacteria in the various colours of a micro-spectrum; there was the accumulation of spermatozoids of mosses in a capillary filled with malic acid, and many other experiments. In fact, all these demonstrations were more thrilling, more impressive, and much more instructive than the slide projections being used today. Of course, they also involved more work.

By following additional lectures (Buder, Stark) in the summer semester of 1919, and through studies and excursions, I had become much more familiar with botany. In the following winter semester (1919-20), I ventured to apply for admittance to a laboratory course in botany for advanced students. It was given *privatissime et gratis* every day in the forenoon. Initially, there were nine participants. Using a good, large microscope, we made detailed studies of subjects which are today still in use in an advanced course; it was only later that this type of work became compulsory. Every day, Pfeffer came along with Stark and checked our work very carefully. He put great value on exact microscopic observations and on exact drawings. Not everyone was able to satisfy his high standards, and after some fourteen days, he would dismiss this or that one from the *privatissime* with a statement like, "If you still can't do this, there is no point in your coming back!" After six weeks, there were only three of us left, Curt Hoffmann (later, Professor for Marine Botany, University of Kiel), Alfred Weis (later, Professor of Biology at the Academy of Pedagogics in Bonn), and myself. Pfeffer was always very kind, but given his serious nature, this never led to a close personal contact. Fortunately, I still have many drawings from those days although quite a few of them were lost and they still remind me of the course.

Work with the microscope was followed by studies in morphology and by experiments in physiology; for the latter, different pieces of equipment, such as clinostats, were used. We were offered many valuable ideas for the future. Toward the end of the semester, we were each given a special assignment. We were to repeat the experiments of recently published studies in morphology or in anatomy, and we were to check the results. This was to give Pfeffer and Stark a better insight into new research work, and at the same time, it was to be a test of our scientific aptitude.

After this semester, Hoffmann and Weis intended to follow other studies. I favoured the idea of continuing to work with Pfeffer and to study for my doctorate. I asked Stark for his opinion, and he suggested that I make an appointment with the *Geheimrat* for the last Friday of the semester. It was the first time I had entered the office of the director of the institute. It was rather large but simple in its furnishings. Pfeffer struck me as looking quite tired. He listened to my request, but then he suggested another meeting in the following week. Regrettably, this meeting never took place. On Saturday morning, I returned to the institute. All of Pfeffer's co-workers had gathered at the south portal of the institute for a group picture with him. I presume that these were the last photos ever taken with Pfeffer. To our sorrow, he died suddenly and unexpectedly the same evening.

By chance, I saw one of the group photos in Japan in 1955; it belonged to one of Pfeffer's former Japanese co-workers. I am attaching it here (fig. 19)

Fig. 19 Pfeffer in a group photo with his co-workers. According to Professor Ullrich, Bonn, this picture was taken on the last day of his life. It is a cut-out from a larger photo owned by Professor Imamura (Japan). Professor Ullrich received this copy through the intermediary of the Goethe Institute in Kyoto. Sitting immediately next to Pfeffer are Professor P. Stark (with glasses) and Professor J. Buder, both named in this book. To the right, behind Pfeffer is Dr. Metzner who was later a Professor at the University in Greifswald.

19

HONOURS AND A SAD END

a) Honours

Pfeffer's accomplishments were given recognition at an early stage. Honours were bestowed on him by German kingdoms and many foreign countries. He was given many medals and decorations, and he was made an honorary member of most academies of sciences and of many scientific societies. Amongst the medals he received was the highest decoration the German Emperor could award, the Prussian *Pour le Merit* [for Sciences and Arts]. A co-worker, H. Fitting, relates how Pfeffer felt about these honours: "He was very pleased in a modest but humanly healthy way. It satisfied the ambition that — as he once said — is needed by any great researcher to drive him on to untiring work. At the same time he felt the deserved pride of a person of prominence who has succeeded in the face of great struggles. He was conscious of his worth and his competence without ever overestimating his own accomplishments."[2a]

Notwithstanding all the honours, Pfeffer thought of success in his research work as being more important. He also gave credit to his co-workers with whom he had close ties. Many of these co-workers came from foreign countries, and they returned to their homelands to continue scientific research after having learned the art from Pfeffer.

b) Pessimism and Depression

The last period of his life did not bring Pfeffer a well-deserved respite from his years of hard and fruitful work. H. Fitting, who knew him well, writes:

> Since he was inclined to brood, he unfortunately did not have the ability to accept old age with a happy and cheerful resignation. With advancing age, he dreaded the idea of leaving the site of his life's work and his lovely home [as director of the botanical gardens and of the Department of Botany he had the use of a large residence in the botanical institute]. For a man still young in spirit and intent on devoting his thoughts to scientific problems, the idea of physical frailty and of dependence on others was most frightening. A life-long inclination to pessimism and to brooding was reinforced with age.

These observations correspond to the impression of others who knew him well. There are frequent remarks about his melancholic moods, his tendency to pessimism, his lack of a sense of humour and a certain degree of misanthropy. In 1912, Pfeffer writes in a letter, "Teaching in the laboratory is not always a pleasure. If it were not for the few students who are truly a pleasure to teach, one could be driven to despair in the face of the combination of stupidity, lack of interest, yes, aversion to learning among most so-called representatives of the intelligentsia. When one stands at the end of a career, such reflections often lead to sad and depressing thoughts."[2a]

In forming an image of the man, one should remember that all reports in print on Pfeffer were written by people who knew him only as an older man. He was already thirty-nine when he married his twenty-two year old bride. He appears in quite a different light when one reads what S. Stippel, a boyhood friend, wrote. Stippel describes an episode that occurred when Pfeffer was still an apprentice: "One day when Willi Pfeffer was in a meadow collecting flowers, a field-warden stopped him and said he was going to charge him for trespassing and for trampling the high grass. Willi, quick of mind, asked the warden, 'Do you not know that a decree of the Landgrave Karl of Hesse authorizes pharmacists to collect medicinal herbs at all times in any field?' The warden fell for the story and went away. . . . . . On the whole, Willi was always cheerful and ready for harmless pranks." About Pfeffer's days as a university student, Stippel writes: "He joined a *Studentenverbindung* [student fraternity] and he was very active in fencing with sabres. It appears he took part in many lively student pranks; he tells me in a letter that so far, he had managed to escape the *Karzer* [prison for students], even though it was a close call at times." It is also known that Pfeffer was an enthusiastic, skilled mountaineer. Over all, he seems to have had an optimistic outlook on life in his youth.

With regard to reports that the older Pfeffer lacked a sense of humour, the question arises as to what represents a sense of humour. It is a subjective concept which has widely different meanings to different nationalities and even in different regions of Germany. That the pessimism of Pfeffer had its origin in his realism becomes evident if one looks at the circumstances of the last years of his life. Pfeffer kept abreast of political happenings, and he applied his analytical thinking to Germany's position in the world. Just as he made clear the statements on scientific questions which others would only accept decades later, he concluded already in 1914 that the war could only end with

Germany's defeat.[73,75] At the same time, he saw no way for Germany to avoid the war, and like most Germans, he was convinced that the fault for the war lay with the other side. He returned the medals that had been conferred on him by countries which had become the enemy, just as most German academics did. However, he was never carried away by the patriotic enthusiasm for the war which was general at the beginning; especially, as he foresaw a tragic end. The very thought of the many former colleagues who were now on the enemy side was enough to depress him.

c) 1918 — 1920

The most bitter blow for Pfeffer was the loss of his son and only child who was killed in action on September 16, 1918, a few weeks before the Armistice. This occurred on the front in France in a sector where American troops were advancing. The loss was made more painful by the fact that his son was officially reported "missing in action." Also, men who had been with his son on a patrol wrote saying that he was severely wounded and had to be left behind. It took the father many months of enquiries and much correspondence before he received a confirmation in mid-1919 that his son was dead.

Even during the war, Pfeffer continued to enjoy great esteem abroad, and witness to this are letters which were exchanged about his son's fate. These include letters between Professor G. Senn of the University of Basel, Switzerland, and Professor B. M. Duggar of the Missouri Botanical Garden, as well as Duggar's correspondence with the American War Department. Both Senn and Duggar had worked under Pfeffer around 1900.

Pfeffer's feelings of depression became more intense in the difficult post-war years in Germany. Food shortages affected him especially, because he refused to eat more than his official ration. Law and order had collapsed in the country, and his savings were rapidly dwindling with the devaluation of the mark. He would have to vacate his official residence, and his prospects of finding a suitable home were slim. Above all, there was the impending end of his scientific career. Here is what he says in a letter written to his daughter-in-law on December 28, 1919:

> A terrible year is coming to an end. It brought us the sad certainty that our beloved Otto has been taken from us forever. It also saw such hopeless developments in our fatherland that we can only look towards the future with trepidation. Let us hope that these fears prove to be wrong, and that the recovery and rebirth of our fatherland takes place as everybody pitches in and works hard .... We were not in the mood to celebrate Christmas .... As far as we are concerned, the New Year will doubtlessly mean unpleasant events. It is apparent that I shall have to retire, and we shall have to vacate the official residence; it is doubtful that we shall be able to find a suitable home. At that, we would have to make do with fewer rooms because we shall not be able to pay much rent. My pension will represent quite a reduction in income. In addition, any income from interest on investments will be very much reduced. First, there is the war-sacrifice surtax which has taken away a part of the capital, and then there is the partial or complete loss in the value of securities which will result in a frightening loss of income from interest. If the collapse of Germany becomes any worse — and unfortunately that is to be expected — then we may very well be reduced to poverty ....

The adjustment to reduced circumstances was even more difficult for Pfeffer's wife. She was very aware of her social position, and she could not deal in a positive manner with the problems presented by a change in life-style. The *Frau Geheimrat* [Madame Privy Councillor] was unable to give her aging husband moral support. At the same time, it pained Pfeffer to know that she was not on particularly good terms with her daughter-in-law, who in her eyes, did not come from a social class that was high enough for her son. Pfeffer, on the other hand, had a good relationship with his daughter-in-law, and he exchanged many warm letters with her until the end. She was the very opposite in personality to her mother-in-law. She was vivacious, enterprising and strong in dealing with the difficulties of life. For instance, in times of food shortages, she did not hesitate to turn to the black market for extra supplies. She revered the old Pfeffer and loved to be in his company. She showed much initiative in making a new life outside of Germany for herself and her son, Pfeffer's only grandchild (born 1917).[75]

d) The Legacy

We have already seen that Pfeffer systematically destroyed letters, manuscripts and documents shortly before his death, (cf. p. 113). There remains a copy of Pfeffer's last will and testament which deals with the disposition of personal possessions. His grandson writes: "He expresses himself with meticulous detail on the disposition of his estate. I noticed that he even made specific reference to the furniture of his mother-in-law, Frau Justine Volk. He wrote that it could no longer be dealt with apart from the Pfeffer belongings because Mrs. Volk had lived in the Pfeffer household for thirty years.... I believe that my grand-father was greatly influenced by two women with strong personalities — his wife and his mother-in-law."[75]

The books in Pfeffer's personal library (11,730 books) were bought by a Mr. Ohara of Japan in 1921. Mr. Ohara

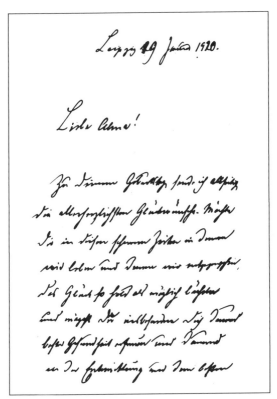

Fig. 20 A page from one of Pfeffer's last letters
(January 19, 1920, written to his daughter-
in-law).

was a respected citizen of Kurashiki and the founder of the
Ohara Institute for Agricultural Research. He donated the
Pfeffer books to the University of Okayama. These books
still exist and are in the library at the Institute of
Agricultural Botany in the town of Kurashiki (fig. 22). Proof
sheets of Pfeffer's writings with corrections in his own
hand are exhibited under glass.

20

IN RETROSPECT

The research performed in Pfeffer's laboratory did not only give a strong incentive to pure scientific research but also to investigations which led to many applications in medicine (osmosis, Theory of Solutions), agriculture, and horticulture. Many have asked, and some still ask, what purpose there is in "playing" with stamens, with trembling leaves, with bending grass shoots, with "frolicking bacteria" (Pfeffer's expression) and with porous pots. The doubters can put their minds at ease. The benefits which resulted from this kind of "playing" far outweighed the financial costs.

This does not mean that funding should be made available to all those who have a project. Not unlike some of Pfeffer's epigones, they will only accomplish what may be called "et cetera work" which will soon be forgotten. Careful selection is needed to decide which scientists merit the means for truly independent research. How this may be done without undue reference to school marks and the like is shown by those who gave Pfeffer his chance. An example of this was the circumstance of his *Habilitation* [appointment to the faculty] of the University of Marburg in 1871. The Faculty of Philosophy took the following position:

Fig. 21 Pfeffer's private library; now kept at the Institute for Agricultural and Biological Sciences of the University of Okayama. It was acquired by a Japanese citizen in a purchase from Pfeffer's widow.

Now that his promotion has been recognized by our faculty, the question of his *general education*, discussed during previous faculty negotiations, can of course no longer be considered. In any case, it seems to us that the accomplishments of Dr. Pfeffer — now under consideration — show an adequate general education in the natural sciences and in mathematics, as well as the required mental acuity and flexibility. He has the formal mental discipline to independently grasp and master a scientific field, not merely the ability to acquire an accumulation of specialized knowledge. This ability for independent thinking is the very objective of a classical education.[2a]

Pfeffer's works and ideas were successful. Many of them gained recognition at an early date, and others had to be rediscovered much later. Even so, it does give satisfaction to find these very recently rediscovered works being quoted in a fair way. That there would be much to be rediscovered was anticipated by Pfeffer's collaborator, E.G. Pringsheim in 1920: "In plant physiology, everything which has yet to be discovered has in a way already been anticipated."

Today, there are even more reasons to speak of the realization of Pfeffer's "prophesies" than when this expression was used by Lidforss in 1915 and E.G. Pringsheim in 1920 (cf. p. 40). However, Pfeffer was not a prophet; rather, he was a researcher who had a remarkable ability to examine and to interpret data.

F. Czapek, a former co-worker and a successor to Pfeffer's post in Leipzig wrote in 1915: "Often, we younger physiologists would give intense thoughts to a problem and painfully evaluate various possibilities. We would then refer to Pfeffer's textbook, only to find in an unexpected spot a clear solution to the problem."

In this context, let us look again at some of the subjects that Pfeffer dealt with. His investigations on energetics and osmosis were soon successfully continued by others. In contrast, it took decades before his work on single-celled organisms was used (with great success) for genetic research. At that, it was generally not remembered that it was Pfeffer who originally proposed this concept. Until quite recently, researchers were not convinced that "the unicellular organism has the ability to do everything" (cf. p. 45). Now, single-celled organisms are used extensively in physiological studies of stimulation and of "senses." In a book published in 1974 and written for non-biologists, S.E. Luria, a Nobel Prize laureate, explains modern biology as it has developed since about 1945. A few quotes illustrate that modern biologists have only now — usually without realizing it — reached the point that Pfeffer's research had already reached. "Thirty years ago, some chemists believed that the unassuming bacterium represented a kind of pouch containing certain catalyzers and substrates, and that it could perform only a few basic processes of physical chemistry. Chemists who held this naive concept were fundamentally mistaken. Bacteria cells have proven to be virtuosos of regulation." Yes, but Pfeffer and his co-workers knew that micro-organisms could perform many complex functions, such as the adaptive formation of enzymes [today called enzyme induction]. Here is another example from Luria's book: "Single-celled protozoa show a degree of complexity in structure and organization which is not achieved by any cell in higher plants or animals." Again, Pfeffer had stated the same thing much earlier, using similar words.

The reality of the endogenous diurnal periodicity (circadian rhythms) was conclusively demonstrated by Pfeffer. Yet, until the mid-twentieth century the concept of an inherited periodicity was considered to belong to the realm of mysticism or metaphysics. He also dealt with circannual rhythms, which he called *autogene Jahresrhythmik*. In recent years, this same subject has been presented as a new discovery at scientific meetings and in publications.

Pfeffer's crowning experimental and intellectual achievement — it was far ahead of its time — is probably his study on the plasma membrane. In his lifetime, only a few appreciated this. One of these was Czapek, who wrote:

Of the many projects involving physics and physiology during his first years in Leipzig, none are more deserving of notice than his studies of the plasma membrane (1890) .... This is the most profoundly thought-out study on the microcosm of the living cell, and it is the best that exists to date regarding the physics of the protoplasm. The intellectual treasures here have barely been exposed; they are significant both for biology and for the science of physics. This is an epilogue to his osmotic investigations, and at the same time it adds in a far-reaching way to the earlier work. Following through on the ingenious writings of the physicist Quincke, Pfeffer gave us the first description of the fundamental phenomena which determine the surface energy of the cell plasma. This leads us to express the hope that more physicists will work just as diligently on questions of cell physiology and thus advance the science of biology. It is to be expected that the study of surface effects will some day lead to the same kind of major results in physics and biology that were achieved when the nature of osmotic pressure was made clear.[1a]

Pfeffer's successes can be attributed in part to the fact that he made good use of different fields of sciences, both on the theoretical and on the practical level. Most of the methods he used were borrowed from other disciplines, although he frequently made his own improvements. In this way, he turned to animal physiology, human physiology, surgery (plaster casts), and of course physics and chemistry.

Unfortunately, German scientists did not take any notice of Pfeffer's call to combine plant and animal physiology as a common field of study. In Germany, botany and zoology were kept neatly separated for many more decades. This was a major reason for Germany's loss of standing in these fields, apart from the political developments after 1933.

21
EPILOGUE

In 1893, Pfeffer spoke to a meeting of the Society of German Naturalists and Physicians on the sensitivity of plants. He had this to say about the quest for new knowledge in sciences:

> Similar to all natural sciences, the research aimed at unlocking the riddles of the workings of life offers an inexhaustible field of activity. If the researcher brilliantly succeeds in bringing light to a previously dark area of science, he will find that in looking out from this newly secured beach his eye is directed to other unknown regions which call on him to embark on a new venture into undiscovered seas. Then, while he battles often hostile elements, he finds that he has to keep adjusting his course towards foreseen and unforeseen goals. Should firm ground be reached again — often in a round-about way — it is just as certain that knowledge will have advanced only a little, even though it may be a significant amount within the boundless expanse of the seas of sciences (1893d).

NOTES

[1a] "Wilhelm Pfeffer zur Feier seines 70. Geburtstages," *Die Naturwissenschaften*, 3, no. 10, pp. 113-140. Contributing authors and titles were as follows: G. Haberlandt, "Wilhelm Pfeffer"; E. Cohen, "Wilhelm Pfeffer und die physikalische Chemie"; F. Czapek, "Die Bedeutung von W. Pfeffers physikalische Forschung für die Pflanzenphysiologie"; H. Kniep, "Wilhelm Pfeffers Bedeutung für die Reizphysiologie"; L. Jost, "Die Bedeutung Wilhelm Pfeffers für die pflanzenphysiologische Technik und Methodik."

[1b] "Pfeffer-Festschrift"(a special edition to honour Pfeffer on his seventieth birthday), *Jahrbücher für wissenschaftliche Botanik*, 56 (1915), 832 pages. A list of Pfeffer's students up to 1915 and their publications is included.

[2a] H. Fitting, "Wilhelm Pfeffer," *Berichte der Deutsch. Bot. Ges.*, 38 (1920), pp. 30-63.

[2b] W. Ruhland, "Wilhelm Pfeffer," *Ber. der Sächsischen Akad. der Wissenschaften*, math.-phys. Kl. 75 (1923), pp. 107-124.

[3] Extracts of letters written in August 1887 by Pfeffer to Strasburger. At the time, Pfeffer expected Strasburger to become his successor at the University of Tübingen. The letters are in the possession of the *Institut für Geschichte der Naturwissenschaften* at the University of Frankfurt.

[4] On von Mohl: R. Braun-Artaria, "Tübinger Gesellschaft um 1860," written around 1900 and copied from *Tübinger Blätter*, 50th annual set, p. 23.

On Goethe: An entry in his diary, dated September 7, 1797. Goethe interrupted a trip to Zürich to go to Tübingen to meet with his publisher, Cotta.

[5] Words by the pastor (of the Reformed Church), Rudolf Mühlhausen at the funeral service, February 5, 1920.

[6] H. Driesch, *Philosophie des Organischen*, 4th ed. (Leipzig, 1928).

J.D. Watson and F. Crick developed the model in 1953. They received the Nobel Prize in 1962.

J.D. Watson, *The Double Helix* (New York, 1968). This book became a bestseller, and it was translated into German.

The "Cargo Cult" started in New Guinea in the 1940s. The Papuan natives were convinced that humans could not produce the objects being used by the white man. They believed that the gods sent aeroplanes filled with these objects.

[7] Z.B.W. Lepeschkin, *Die Kolloidchemie der Protoplasmas* (Berlin: Springer, 1924). The first clear proof of the existence of a distinct plasma membrane resulted from micro-injection experiments, and they were undertaken by Chambers and Reznikoff (J. gen. Physiol., 8, 1926), 369.

[8] It is interesting to compare the to and fro, and the ponderings and doubts encountered in Pfeffer's *Handbuch* with the ready optimism of J. Loeb's *Vorlesungen über die Dynamik der Lebenserscheinungen* (German translation, Leipzig, 1906). As an example, there is the following statement about the effect of light in the phototropism of plants: "Regardless of the nature of this effect, it is certain that it causes a reduction in the stretching of the stem, or perhaps a direct shortening or contraction, comparable to that of animals ...." Or again, when Loeb speaks of tropism in animals, he writes, "This sketch of tropism should suffice to show that simple physical-chemical conditions are the basis for appropriate, instinctive actions of animals."

Here, there are none of the "innumerable ifs and buts"which drove Haberlandt "nearly to desperation"(G. Haberlandt, Recollections, Berlin, 1933).

[9] Pfeffer's theses, written by hand, as well as printed versions of these are kept in the archives of Hessia in Marburg.

[10] Quoted by Th. Schmucker, *Geschichte der Biologie* (Gottingen: Vandenhoeck und Ruprecht, 1936).

[11] It may be noted that the romantic philosophy of nature was to a degree an over-reaction to concepts of the eighteenth century which did not see a boundary between animate and inanimate matter.

[12] Pfeffer (1867-1869a; 1871b,d,e). The distant relative in Chur was an "uncle" Theobald, and Pfeffer named a species of moss in his honour. According to a personal communication from Professor Mägdefrau, Munich, the liverwort *Didymodon theobaldii* is identical with *Desmatodon latifolius (Hedw.) Bridel* var. *muticus Bridel*.

[13] In his *Osmotische Untersuchungen* Pfeffer described Nägeli's pioneering achievements in detail.

Pfeffer eventually (1897) gave up the concept of tagmas in favour of the concept of micelles, especially after miscelles were characterized as complexes of molecules.

H. Staudiner, *Makromolekulare Chemie und Biologie* (Basel, 1947).

Staudinger's first publication on macromolecules appeared in 1920 (Berichte Deutsche Chem. Ges. 53, p. 1073).

Developments from Nägli to the beginning of World War II are described in A. Frey-Wyssling, *Submikroskopische Morphologie des Protoplasmas und seiner Derivate*, 2nd ed. (Berlin, 1938).

[14] Pfeffer's letters are in the archives of the University of Tübingen. A detailed history of the events surrounding the Tübinger greenhouses is given by Elke von Schulz in the journal *Attempo*, 33/34, 1969. After the old botanical garden was closed (1967), there was a citizens' drive, a raising of funds, and a competition for ideas to preserve the greenhouses. Yet, in the end, they were torn down because of the high costs of maintenance.
[15] Professor J. Buder in his funeral oration on behalf of the staff of the Botanical Institute, February 5, 1920.
[16] Pfeffer (1873b, 1874b, 1875b).
[17] In the preamble to Pfeffer (1877a).
[18] J. Sachs, *Lehrbuch der Botanik*, 4th ed. (Leipzig: W. Engelmann, 1874).
[19] Morses' many words are brought together in H.N. Morse, The *Osmotic Pressure of Aqueous Solutions* (Washington 1914). Even in recent books, Dutrochet is often called the discoverer of osmosis. But Pfeffer (1876) writes, "Osmosis was already discovered in the last century (1748) by Nollet, but so little attention was paid to this that the rediscovery by Fischer (1812) was taken as a first. In other respects, these scientists, and also Parrot who built on Nollet, only reported facts, but they did not present research guided by leading concepts to achieve a deeper understanding. We find this for the first time with Dutrochet who reported on numerous experiments in publications between 1826 and 1837, and who attempted nearly as many explanations of the phenomenon. This author was fully aware of the physiological significance of these explanations."
[20] Cohen, note 1a.
[21] Many historical references are found in P.H.W.A.M. de Veer, *Leven en werk van Hugo de Vries* (Groningen: Wolters-Noordhoff, 1969).
W. Hofmeister, Die Lehre von der Pflanzenzelle (Leipzig: W. Engelmann, 1967), p. 3.
[22] S. Colla, "Die kontraktile Zelle der Pflanzen," *Protoplasma-Monographien*, 10 (Berlin, 1937).
T. Sibaoka, "Physiology of Rapid Movements in Higher Plants," Ann. Rev. Plant Physiol., 20 (1969), pp. 165-184.
[23] Pfeffer (1890c).
[24] G. de Vries, "Plasmolytische Studien über die Wand der Vacuolen," Jahrb. f. wiss. Bot., 16 (1885), pp. 464-598. Chromatophores: pigmented bodies, especially chloroplasts which contain chlorophyll.
[25] H. Drawert, "Vitalfärbung und Vitalfluorochromierung pflanzlicher Zellen und Gewebe," *Protoplasmatologia*, Vol. II, D, 3 (1968), pp. 1-749.
Plasmodia: a mass of protoplasm formed by the flowing together of cells containing many nuclei but no cell walls.

[26] R.A. Manson, ed., *Biomembranes*, 3 volumes (New York-London: Plenum Press, 1971-1972). *The Journal of Membrane Biology*. An International Journal for Studies on the Structure, Function and Genesis of Biomembranes. A suitable book for introduction to the subject is D.F. Hoelzl and H.G. Knüfermann, *Plasmamembran* Berlin-Heidelberg-New York, 1973).

[27] On the development of these theories compare P.R. Collander, "Ernest Overton (1863-1933) A Pioneer to Remember," *Leopoldina*, 3, 8/9 (1962/1963), pp. 242-254. Overton's most important work occurred in the period 1895-1907.

For decades, researchers in the field of permeability largely ignored Pfeffer's warnings and Overton's work. Already in 1896, Overton stated, "These examples should adequately demonstrate that the cell's intake and delivery of complexes in solution are not always due to purely osmotic processes; instead, the absorption and discharge of matter by living cells may be caused by another mechanism (set in motion by and regulated by the vital actions of the cells) which may, in given cases, move dissolved substances in a direction exactly opposite to the one it should have followed, if diffusion alone were the cause." *Vierteljahrsschrift Naturforsch. Ges.*, 41 (Zürich: 1896), pp. 383-406.

Lidforss, "Algemeine Biologie," *Kultur der Gengenwart*, part 3, sect. 4 (Leipzig and Berlin: 1915).

[28] J. Monod and F. Jacob, Cold Spring Harbor Symposia on Quantitative Biol., 26 (1961), pp. 389-401. General conclusions: Teleonomic mechanisms in cellular metabolism, growth and differentiation.

[29] Pfeffer (1890b), also (1890e, 1886a, 1886e, 1897).

[30] W. Engelmann, "Zur Biologie der Schizomyceten," *Archiv. f. d. ges. Physiol.*, 26 (1881), pp. 537-545. E. Stahl, "Zur Biologie der Myxomyceten," *Bot. Zeitung*, 40 (1884), pp. 146-155, 162-175. Myxomycete: Slime moulds, flagellata.

[31] Pfeffer (1884, 1888a, 1888b, 1893d). Cit. from (1893d).

[32] An article by H. Kniep explains the debates which took place at the time. H. Kniep, "Botanische Analogien zur Psychophysik," *Fortschritte der Psychologie und ihrer Anwendungen*, 4 (1916), pp. 81-119.

[33] Occasionally, the expressions "perception"and "reception"are used for separate components of a reaction to stimulation. This distinction was not made in the older literature. In the newer literature, the term "reception" is most common.

[34] J. Adler, "Chemotaxis in *Escherichia coli*," in *Behaviour of Micro-Organisms*, ed. A. Pérez-Miravete (London-New York: Plenum Press, 1973), pp. 1-14.

Cf. H.C. Berg and D.A. Brown, "Chemotaxis in *Escherichia coli* analysed by three-dimensional tracking," *Nature*, 239 (1972), pp. 500-504. In these two works, Pfeffer is one of the few authors quoted.

[35] Massart et Bordet, Soc. Roy. de Sc. med. et nat. de Bruxelles (1890).

[36] Cf. B.B. Diehn, "Phototaxis and Sensory Transduction in Euglena," *Science*, 181 (1973), pp. 1009-1015. The author's studies with single-celled flagellata led him to the question: "Is the system capable of permanent or transitory modification through repeated response, that is, does it exhibit phenomena analogous to learning and memory of higher organisms?" Thus, the question which had been raised before is again asked, especially by H.S. Jennings. H.S. Jennings, *Das Verhalten der niederen Organismen* (Leipzig und Berlin, 1910), trans. from Engl. ed. (1905).

[37] N. Tsang, R. Macnab, D.E. Koshland, *Science*, 181 (1973), pp. 60-63.

[38] De Candolle, cf. Pfeffer (1893d). Prototropism: bending caused by the action of light from one side (cf. fig. 17). Geotropism: bending due to gravity.

[39] J.R. Mayer, "Über Auslösung," in a special supplement of the *Staatsanzeiger für Württemberg*, 1, 15 (Jan. 1876).

[40] Pfeffer (1885a and 1904).

[41] G. Haberlandt, *Sinnesorgane im Pflanzenreich zur Perzeption mechanischer Reize*, 2nd ed. (Leipzig, 1906).

G. Haberlandt, *Die Lichtsinnesorgane der Blätter*, (Leipzig, 1905).

[42] M.J. Jaffe and A.W. Galston, "The Physiology of Tendriles," Ann. Rev. Plant Physiol., 19 (1968), pp. 417-433.

[43] This was confirmed in later research. Today, plant physiologists are again very involved in research on these primary functions. Although significant questions still remain, it has been found that there is a great similarity between the various organisms, from the single-celled organism to the higher animals.

[44] Cf. Katz (1898) and Kylin (1914). Kylin drew a distinction between "qualitative"and "quantitative"enzyme induction.

[45] Pfeffer (1904), p. 366. Such oscillations about equilibrium are now acknowledged for various movements in plants. Autogenous: induced by internal factors (in translation used term, endogenous).

[46] Czapek, note 1a. Aleurone: protein substance stored in plants.

[47] Rubner, Z. f. Biol., NF 12 (1894).

Lanlanié, Arch. de Physiologie (1898), p. 748.

Atwater, Ergebn. d. Physiol., III, 1 (1904), p. 497.

Meyerhof, Pflügers Archiv. f. Physiol., 146 (1912), p. 181 ff.

⁴⁸ Pfeffer (1897) pp. 523, 541. It is here that we find the reference to Pasteur. In 1875, Pflüger had already expressed himself in a manner similar to Pfeffer. Boysen Jensen is one of the early researchers in this field at the beginning of the century. Further advances are connected with the names Embden, Euler, Meyerhof, Neuberg, and Warburg.
⁴⁹ Pfeffer (1892a, 1897).
Warburg, *Med. Wochenschr.*, 47 (1912).
Meyerhof, *Abh. d. Fries'schen Schule*, N.F. 4 (1914) p. 429 ff.
⁵⁰ R.L. Satter and A.W. Galston in *BioScience*, 23 (1973), pp. 407-418.
⁵¹ M. de Mairan, *Acad. Roy. Soc.* (Paris, 1729) p. 35.
⁵² Ch. Darwin, *Das Bewegungsvermogen der Pflanzen* (Stuttgart, 1881).
A. Weismann, *Arch. Rassenbiol.*, 3, 1 (1906).
⁵³ R. Semon, *Biolog. Zentralbl.*, 25 (1905), p. 241 and 28 (1908), p. 225.
A. Weismann, *Arch. Rassenbiol.*, 3, 1 (1906).
⁵⁴ K. Lorenz, *Die acht Todsünden der zivilisierten Menschheit* (München, 1973).
K. Lorenz, *Die Rückseite des Spiegels* (München, 1973). It is evident that Loeb made a much wider use of the concept of "tropism" than the botanists.
⁵⁵ F.v.P. Schrank, *Vom Pflanzenschlafe und von anverwandten Erscheinungen bei Pflanzen* (Ingolstadt, 1792).
⁵⁶ C.P. Richter, *A Behavioristic Study of the Activity of the Rat*, Comp. Psychol. Monogr. 1, 1 (1922).
⁵⁷ Synopsis - E. Bünning, *The Physiological Clock*, rev. 3rd ed. (New York, 1973). Charles Darwin (and other scientists) tried in vain to discover an adaptive value for the diurnal periodicity of leaf movements. The answer seems to be that the leaf has to respond to the rapid change in the intensity of the light rays which hit the leaf surface at twilight. This is of importance in day length measurements, as in the case of photoperiodic reactions.
⁵⁸ Anthonia Kleinhoonte, *De door het licht geregelte autonome bewegingen der Canavalia-bladern*, Diss. (Utrecht, 1928). German translation in Arch. neerl. Sc. exact. nat. Ser III B, tome V (1929), pp. 1-110.
⁵⁹ K.v. Goebel in a letter to G. Karsten (1921). Quoted in E. Bergdolt, *Karl von Goebel* (Berlin, 1940).
⁶⁰ Darwin also drew attention to other correlations in plant movements. For instance, he spoke of the root tip having a "brain function." Cf. Pfeffer (1894a and b).
⁶¹ D. Müller in an obituary for Boysen Jensen; translated from *Botan. Tidsskrift*, 55 (Copenhagen, 1960), pp. 325-336.
⁶² Pfeffer's initial skepticism is easy to understand. It was assumed that a "stimulus transmission" was involved, as Fitting's (Pfeffer's

student) earlier experiments seemed to prove that transmission was only possible along living cells. However, this was found to be in error, and in the end, Fitting himself, congratulated Boysen Jensen. Later, it was determined that hormone diffusion and not stimulus transmission was involved.

[63] Von Goebel in a letter to O.F. Bower; E. Bergdolt.[59]

[64] F.W. Went, "Wuchsstoff und Wachstum," *Rec. Trav. bot. néerl.*, 25 (1928), pp. 1-116.

[64] It is now known that the growth substance is indolyl-d-acetic acid, a relatively simple compound, and one that is easy to produce on a commercial scale. A synthetic compound, 2,4-dichlorophenoxy acetic acid is similar in action to the natural auxin. It is produced on a large scale as a herbicide for broadleaf plants growing on lawns and in grain fields. The subject is summarized in L.J. Audus, *Plant Growth Substances*, 3rd ed., several volumes (London, 1972).

[66] E. Pringsheim, *Julius Sachs* (Jena, 1932).

[67] Von Goebel in a letter to J. Sachs; E. Bergdolt.[59]

[68] Von Goebel in a letter to G. Karsten; E. Bergdolt.[59]

[69] B.M. Duggar, Missouri Botanical Garden, in a letter of June 12, 1919 to Colonel Hunt, United States Army, Washington, D.C. Cf. p. concerning the purpose of the letter.

[70] C. Correns in his funeral oration, February 5, 1920.

[71] H. Tamiya, "Keita Shibata," *Ber. Deutsch. Bot. Ges.*, 68a, (1955), pp. 13-16.

S. Hattori, Keita Shibata (1876-1947), *Bot. Magaz.*, 62, (Tokyo, 1949).

[72] B. Holzmann, *Eduard Strasburger. Stein Leben, seine Zeit und sein Werk*, Diss. (Frankfurt/Main, 1967).

[73] G. Haberlandt, *Erinnerungen* (Berlin, 1933).

[74] H.R. Oppenheimer, in *Palestine Journal of Botany and Horticultural Science* (1935). In writing to me [Prof. Bünning, Professor M. Evenari of Jerusalem said in regard to this question: "Unfortunately, we cannot ask Professor Oppenheimer on what he based his claim of a Jewish descent for Pfeffer. Oppenheimer died three years ago. In regard to . . . Pfeffer, I personally was not sure, but I distinctly remember that the two of us discussed the question. As far as I remember after such a long time, he stated that he had seen relevant documents, and that a Jewish descent. . . was not generally known because, as in many other cases, baptized Jews tried to keep the secret of their origin."

[75] Personal communications of the grandson, Dr. H.W. Pfeffer, Ottawa (letters, documents and family recollections).

[76] S.E. Luria, *Leben das unvollendete Experiment* (Münich-Zürich: R. Piper, 1974).

PUBLICATIONS BY PFEFFER

Compiled by H. Fitting[2a]

1865 Über einige Derivate des Glyzerins und dessen Überführung in Allylen. Inaug.-Diss. Göttingen. 30 Seiten.

1867 Aus der Mooswelt der Alpen. Jahrb. d. Schweiz. Alpenklubs. Bd. 4. S. 454-477.

1868 a) Bryologische Reisebilder aus dem Adula. Jahresber. der Nat. Forsch. Gesellschaft Graubündens. Neue Folge. Bd. 13. S. 44-82.

1868 b) *Didymodon Theobaldii*, eine neue Moosart. Ebenda. Bd. 13. S. 83 bis 88. 2 Taf.

1868 c) Zwei Mißbildungen von Laubmoosfrüchten. Ebenda. Bd. 13. S. 150 bis 157.

1869 a) Über Bildung von Korolle und Androeceum der Primulaceen. Sitzungsber. d. Naturf. Freunde Berlin 21. Dez. 1869; auch Bot. Zeitung Bd. 28. 1870. S. 143.

1869 b) Bryogeographische Studien aus den rhätischen Alpen. Neue Denkschrift d. allg. schweiz. Gesellsch. f. d. gesamt. Naturwiss. Zürich 1871. 142 S.

1871 a) Die Wirkung farbigen Lichtes auf die Zersetzung der Kohlensäure in Pflanzen. Arb. d. Bot. Institutes Würzburg. Bd. 1. S. 1-76; auch sep. als Habil.-Schrift Marburg 1871.

1871 b) Studien über Symmetrie und specifische Wachstumsursachen. Ebenda. Bd. 1. S. 77-98.

1871 c) Zur Frage über die Wirkung farbigen Lichtes auf die Kohlensäurezersetzung. Botan. Zeitung. Bd. 29. S. 319-323.

1871 Über die Embryobildung höherer Kryptogamen. Sitzungsber. d. Gesellschaft z. Beförderung d. gesamt. Naturwiss. Marburg 1871. S. 6 ff.

1871 e) Entwicklung des Keimes der Gattung *Selaginella*. Bot. Abhandl. Herausg. von Hanstein. Bd. 1. Heft 4. 80 S.

1871 f) Über geformte Eiweißkörper und die Wanderung der Eiweißstoffe beim Keimen der Samen. Sitzungsber. d. Gesellsch. z. Beförderung d. gesamt. Naturwiss. Marburg. S. 69 ff.; auch Bot. Zeitung. Bd. 30. S. 276-279, 299-302.

1872 a) Über die Wirkung der Spektralfarben auf die Kohlensäurezersetzung in Pflanzen. Ebenda. S. 65; auch Annalen d. Physik u. Chemie. Bd. 148. S. 86-99.

1872 b) Die Wirkung der Spektralfarben auf die Kohlensäurezersetzung in Pflanzen. Bot. Zeitung. Bd. 30. S. 425-439, 449-462, 465-472.

1872 c) Bemerkungen zu A. Schmidt Mitteilungen über die Mittellinie der Naviculeen. Tagebl. d. 45. Versammlung deutsch. Naturf. u. Ärzte. Leipzig. S. 142; auch Bot. Zeitung. Bd. 30. S. 743.

1872 d) Über das Öffnen und Schließen der Blüthen. Tageblatt d. 45. Versammlung deutsch. Naturf. u. Ärzte. Leipzig. S. 72 ff.; auch Botanische Zeitung. Bd. 30. S. 733.

1872 e) Über Wasserbewegung. Im Anschluß an einen Vortrag von Sorauer. Tageblatt d. 45. Versamml. deutsch. Naturf. u. Ärzte. Leipzig. S. 144; auch Bot. Zeitung. Bd. 30. S. 749.

1872 f) Untersuchungen über Reizbewegung. Sitzber. d. Gesellsch. z. Beförd. d. gesamt. Naturwiss. Marburg. S. 129; auch Bot. Zeitung. Bd. 30. S. 877-882.

1872 g) Zur Blüthenentwicklung der Primulaceen und Ampelideen. Jahrb. f. wiss. Bot. Bd. 8. S. 194-214.

1872 h) Untersuchungen über die Proteïnkörner und die Bedeutung des Asparagins beim Keimen der Samen. Ebenda. S. 429-574.

1873 a) Über Öffnen und Schließen der Blüthen. Sitzber. d. Gesellsch. z. Beförd. d. gesamt. Naturwiss. Marburg. S. 1; auch Bot. Zeitung. Bd. 31. S. 239-240, 247-250.

1873 b) Physiologische Untersuchungen. Leipzig. 216 S.

1873 c) Über die Beziehung des Lichtes zur Rückbildung von Eiweißstoffen aus dem beim Keimen gebildeten Asparagin. Tagebl. d. 46. Versamml. Deutsch. Naturf. u. Ärzte. Wiesbaden. S. 67 ff.; auch Bot. Zeitung. Bd. 32. S. 235.

1873 d) Über die Beziehung des Lichtes zur Regeneration von Eiweißstoffen aus dem beim Keimungsproceß gebildeten Asparagin. Monatsber. d. Berlin. Akad. d. Wiss. 1873. Berlin 1874. S. 780.

1873 e) Über Fortpflanzung des Reizes bei *Mimosa pudica*. Jahrb. f. wiss. Bot. Bd. 9. S. 308-326.

1874 a) Die Ölkörper der Lebermoose. Flora. Bd. 32. S. 1-25.

1874 b) Über periodische Bewegungen der Blätter. Sitzber. d. Niederrhein. Gesellsch. f. Nat. und Heilkunde. Bonn.

1874 c) Hesperidin, ein Bestandtheil einiger Hesperideen. Bot. Zeitg. Bd. 32. S. 481 ff.

1874 d) Die Produktion organischer Substanz in der Pflanze. Landwirt. Jahrb. Bd. 3. S. 1-16.

1874 e) Die Bildung stickstoffhaltiger Substanz in der Pflanze. Ebenda. Bd. 3. S. 437-448.

1875 a) Heckels Ansichten über den Mechanismus der Reizbewegungen. Botan. Zeitung. Bd. 33. S. 289-291.

1875 b) Die periodischen Bewegungen der Blattorgane. Leipzig. 176 S.

1875 c) Über die Bildung des Primordialschlauches. Sitzber. d. Niederrh. Gesellsch. f. Nat. u. Heilkunde. S. 198; auch Botan. Zeitg. Bd. 33. S. 660 und Bd. 34. S. 74.

1875 d) Über das Zustandekommen eines hohen osmotischen Druckes in Pflanzenzellen durch endosmotische Wirkung. Ebenda Sitzungsber. S. 276; auch Botan. Zeitung. Bd. 84. S. 75.

1875 e) Über die Entstehung hoher hydrostatischer Druckkräfte in Pflanzenzellen. Tagebl. der 48. Versamml. deutsch. Naturf. u. Ärzte in Graz. 1875; auch Botan. Zeitung. Bd. 33. S. 733.

1876 a) Besprechung von "Heckel, E.: Du mouvement végétal. Paris 1875" in Bot. Zeitg. Bd. 34. S. 9.

1876 b) Die Wanderung der organischen Baustoffe in der Pflanze. Landwirtsch. Jahrb. Bd. 5. S. 87-130.

1877 a) Osmotische Untersuchungen. Studien zur Zellmechanik. Leipzig. 236 S.

1877 b) Über fleischfressende Pflanzen und über die Ernährung durch Aufnahme organischer Stoffe überhaupt. Landw. Jahrb. Bd. 6. S. 969 bis 998.

1878 Das Wesen und die Bedeutung der Athmung in der Pflanze. Ebenda. Bd. 7. S. 805-834.

1881 Pflanzenphysiologie. Ein Handbuch des Stoffwechsels und Kraftwechsels in der Pflanze. Bd. 1. 383 S. Bd. 2. 474 S.

1883 Locomotorische Richtungsbewegungen durch chemische Reize. Ber. der Deutsch. Bot. Gesellsch. Bd. 1. S. 524-533.

1884 Lokomotorische Richtungsbewegungen durch chemische Reize. Untersuch. aus d. Bot. Instit. Tübingen. Bd. 1. S. 363-482.

1885 a) Zur Kenntnis der Kontaktreize. Ebenda. Bd. 1. S. 483-535.

1885 b) Über intramolekulare Athmung (unter Zugrundelegung der von Dr. W.P. Wilson ausgeführten Versuche). Ebenda. Bd. 1. S. 636-685.

1886 a) Über Aufnahme von Anilinfarben in lebende Zellen. Ebenda. Bd. 2. S. 179-331.

1886 b) Kritische Besprechung von "De Vries: Plasmolytische Studien üb. die Wand der Vacuolen etc." Botan. Zeitung. Bd. 44. S. 114-125.

1886 c) Über Stoffaufnahme in die lebende Zelle. Tagebl. d.
59. Versamml. deutsch. Naturf. u. Ärzte. Berlin. S. 302;
auch Ber. d. Deutsch. Bot. Gesellsch. Bd. 4. S. XXX.

1887 Bezugsquelle und Preis einiger Apparate. Botan. Ztg.
Bd. 45. S. 27-31.

1888 a) Über chemotaktische Bewegungen von Bakterien,
Flagellaten und Volvocineen. Untersuch. aus d.
Botan. Institut Tübingen. Bd. 2. S. 582-661.

1888 b) Über Anlockung von Bakterien und einigen
anderen Organismen durch chemische Reize.
Humboldt. Bd. 7. Heft 6.

1889 a) Loew und Bokornys Silberreduction in Pflanzenzellen. Flora. Bd. 47. S. 46-54.

1889 b) Über Oxydationsvorgänge in lebenden Zellen. Ber.
d. Deutsch. Bot. Gesellsch. Bd. 7. S. 82-89.

1889 c) Beiträge zur Kenntnis der Oxydationsvorgänge in
lebenden Zellen. Abhandl. d. math.-phys. Kl. d.
königl. sächs. Gesellsch. d. Wiss. Leipzig. Bd. 15. S.
375-518.

1889 d) Üb. die im bot. Institut angestellt. Untersuchungen
des Herrn P. Eschenhagen betr. den Einfluß der
Concentration des Nährmediums auf das Wachstum
der Schimmelpilze. Ber. d. kgl. sächs. Gesellsch. d.
Wiss. Math.-phys. Kl. Leipzig. Bd. 41. S. 343-346.

1890 a) Ein neuer heizbarer Objekttisch, nebst Bemerkungen über einige Heizeinrichtungen. Zeitschr. f. wiss.
Mikroskopie, Bd. 7. S. 433-449.

1890 b) Über Aufnahme und Ausgabe ungelöster Körper.
Abhandl. d. math.-phys. Kl. d. kgl. sächs. Gesellsch. d.
Wiss. Leipzig. Bd. 16. S. 149 bis 183.

1890 c) Zur Kenntniß der Plasmahaut und der Vacuolen
nebst Bemerkungen über den Aggregatzustand des
Protoplasmas und über osmotische Vorgänge.
Ebenda. Bd. 16. S. 185-344.

1891 a) Über die von Herrn Dr. Wehmer im botan. Institut ausgeführten Untersuchungen betr.: Die Bildungsbedingungen der Oxalsäure in Pilzen. Ber. d. kgl. sächs. Gesellsch. d. Wiss. Math.-phys. Kl. Leipzig. Bd. 43. S. 24-27.

1891 b) Untersuchungen von R. Hegler: Über den Einfluß von Zugkräften auf die Festigkeit und die Ausbildung mechanischer Gewebe in Pflanzen. Ebenda. Bd. 43. S. 638-643.

1892 a) Studien zur Energetik der Pflanze. Abhandl. d. math.-phys. Kl. der sächs. Gesellsch. d. Wiss. Leipzig. Bd. 18. S. 151-276.

1892 b) Über Anwendung des Gipsverbandes für pflanzenphysiologische Studien. Ber. d. kgl. sächs. Gesellsch. d. Wiss. Math.-phys. Kl. Leipzig. Bd. 44. S. 538-542.

1893 a) Druck- und Arbeitsleistung durch wachsende Pflanzen. Abhandl. d. math.-phys. Kl. d. sächs. Gesellsch. d. Wiss. Leipzig. Bd. 20. S. 235 bis 474.

1893 b) Über Untersuchungen des Herrn Dr. Miyoshi aus Tokio betr. die chemotropischen Bewegungen von Pilzfäden. Ber. d. kgl. sächs. Gesellsch. d. Wiss. Math.-phys. Kl. Leipzig. Bd. 45. S. 319-324.

1893 c) Über die Ursachen der Entleerung der Reservestoffe aus Samen auf Grund der Untersuchungen von Herrn B. Hansteen. Ebenda. S. 421 bis 428.

1893 d) Die Reizbarkeit der Pflanzen. Verhandl. d. Gesellschaft deutsch. Naturf. u. Ärzte in Nürnberg. Allg. Teil. S. 1-31.

1893 e) L'irritabilité chez les plantes. Revue scientifique. Paris. Bd. 52. S. 737 bis 744.

1893 f) De l'irritabilité chez les plantes. Archives d. scienc. physiques et natur. Genève. Bd. 30. S. 397-421.

1893 g) Über Arbeitsleistungen der Pflanzen. Verhandl. d. Gesellsch. deutsch. Naturf. und Ärzte. 65. Versammlung. Nürnberg 1893. Bd. II, 1. S. 145.

1893 h) Herausgabe von Koelreuters Vorläuf. Nachricht von einigen das Geschlecht usw. betr. Versuchen usw. Nebst Biographie und Würdigung der Verdienste des Verf. Ostwalds Klassiker d. exakt. Wiss. Nr. 41.

1894 a) Über die geotropische Sensibilität der Wurzelspitze nach von Dr. Czapek im Leipz. Bot. Institute angestellt. Untersuchungen. Ber. d. kgl. sächs. Gesellsch. d. Wiss. Leipzig. Math.-phys. Kl. Bd. 46. S. 168 bis 172.

1894 b) Geotropic sensitiveness of the root-tip. Annals of Botany. Bd. 8. S. 317-320.

1895 a) Ein Zimmer mit konstanten Temperaturen. Ber. d. Deutsch. Bot. Gesellsch. Bd. 13. S. 49-54.

1895 b) Berichtigung über die correlative Beschleunigung des Wachsthums in der Wurzelspitze. Jahrb. f. wiss. Botanik. Bd. 27. S. 481-483.

1895 c) Über Election organischer Nährstoffe. Ebenda. Bd. 28. S. 205-268.

1895 d) Über ein Zimmer mit konstanten Temperaturen. Ber. d. kgl. sächs. Gesellsch. d. Wiss. Math.-phys. Kl. Bd. 47. S. 52.

1895 e) Über elektiven Stoffwechsel. Berl. d. kgl. sächs. Gesellsch. d. Wiss. Math.-phys. Kl. Leipzig. Bd. 47. S. 324-328.

1896 a) Einleitende Betrachtungen zu einer Physiologie des Stoffwechsels und Kraftwechsels in der Pflanze. Akad. Dissertat. Leipzig. 49 S.

1896 b) Über die vorübergehende Aufhebung der Assimilationsfähigkeit in Chlorophyllkörpern auf Grund d. im bot. Institut von Herrn Ewart ausgeführten Untersuchungen. Ber. d. kgl. sächs. Gesellsch. d. Wiss. Math.-phys. Kl. Leipzig. Bd. 48. S. 311-314.

1896 c) Über die lockere Bindung von Sauerstoff in gewissen Bakterien, welche von Herrn Ewart untersucht wurde. Ebenda. S. 379-383.

1896 d) Über die Steigerung der Athmung und Wärmeproduction nach Verletzung lebenskräftiger Pflanzen; traumatische Reaktionen, welche von Herrn Dr. H.M. Richards näher studiert wurden. Ebenda. S. 384 bis 389.

1896 e) Über die im botan. Institut ausgeführten Untersuchungen des Herrn Townsend über den Einfluβ des Zellkerns auf die Bildung der Zellhaut. Ebenda. S. 505-512.

1896 f) Über regulatorische Bildung von Diastase auf Grund der von Herrn Dr. Katz im botan. Institut angestellten Untersuchungen. Ebenda. S. 513-518.

1897 Pflanzenphysiologie. Ein Handbuch der Lehre vom Stoffwechsel und Kraftwechsel in der Pflanze. 2. völlig umgearbeitete Aufl. Bd. 1. Leipzig. 620 S.

1898 The nature and significance of functional metabolism in the plant. Proceed. Royal Soc. London. Bd. 63. Croonian lecture. S. 93-101.

1899 Über die Erzeugung und die physiologische Bedeutung der Amitose nach Untersuchungen des Herrn A. Nathanson. Ber. d. kgl. sächs. Gesellsch. d. Wiss. Math.-phys. Kl. Leipzig. Bd. 51. S. 4-12.

1900 Die Anwendung des Projectionsapparates zur Demonstration von Lebensvorgängen. Jahrb. f. wiss. Bot. Bd. 35. S. 711-745.

1900/06 The Physiology of Plants, transl. by Ewart. Oxfort. Bd. 1. 1900. Bd. 2. 1903/06.

1904 Pflanzenphysiologie. Handbuch usw. Bd. 2. 2. Auflg. 986 S.

1905/12 Physiologie végétale, trad. par J. Friedel. Bd. 1. 1905. Bd. 2. 1908 bis 1912.

1907 a) Untersuchungen über die Entstehung der Schlafbewegungen der Blattorgane. Abhandl. d. math.-phys. Kl. d. kgl. sächs. Gesellsch. d. Wiss. Leipzig. Bd. 30. S. 259-472.

1907 b) Über die Ursache der Schlafbewegung. Naturwiss. Rundschau. Bd. 22. S. 618.

1907 c) Über die Entstehung der Schlafbewegungen bei Pflanzen. Tagebl. der 79. Versammlung deutsch. Naturf. und Ärzte in Dresden. Teil II, 1. S. 219.

1908 Die Entstehung der Schlafbewegungen bei Pflanzen. Biolog. Zentralblatt. Bd. 28. S. 389-415.

1909 Die botanischen Institute. Festschr. z. 500. Universitätsjubiläum Leipzig. 18 Seiten. 3 Pläne.

1911 Der Einfluβ von mechanischer Hemmung und von Belastung auf die Schlafbewegung. Abhandl. d. math.-phys. Kl. d. kgl. sächs. Gesellsch. d. Wiss. Bd. 32. S. 163-295.

1914 Carl Chun. Nekrolog. gesprochen in der öffentl. Gesamtsitzung beider Klassen d. kgl. sächs. Gesellsch. d. Wiss. Leipzig, am 4. Nov. 1914. Ber. d. math.-phys. Kl. d. kgl. sächs. Gesellsch. d. Wiss. Leipzig. Bd. 66. 15 S.

1915 Beiträge zur Kenntnis der Entstehung der Schlafbewegungen. Ebenda. Bd. 34. S. 1-154.

1916 Über die Verbreitung der haptotropischen Reaktionsfähigkeit und das Wesen der Tastreizbarkeit. Berichte d. math.-phys. Kl. d. kgl. sächs. Gesellsch. d. Wiss. Leipzig. Bd. 68. S. 93-120.

PUBLICATIONS BY COLLABORATORS

Publications on research performed in Pfeffer's laboratory and under his guidance. (For the authors who are not from Germany, the country of origin or the place of residence is indicated.)

Andrews, F.A. (USA): Über die Wirkung der Zentrifugalkraft auf Pflanzen. Diss. Leipzig 1903. — Jahrb. f. wiss. Bot. 38 (1903)

Bachmann, F.: Beitrag zur Kenntnis obligat anaerober Bakterien. Diss. Leipzig 1912. — Centralblatt f. Bakteriol. Abt. II, 36 (1912)

Ball, O.M. (USA): Der Einfluß von Zug auf die Ausbildung von Festigungsgewebe. Diss. Leipzig 1904. — Jahrb. f. wiss. Bot. 39 (1904)

Bäßler, F.: Über den Einfluß des Dekapitierens auf die Richtung der Blätter an orthotropen Sprossen. Diss. Leipzig 1909. — Botan. Zeitung 67 (1909)

Bartetzko, H.: Untersuchungen über das Erfrieren von Schimmelpilzen. Diss. Leipzig 1909. — Jahrb. f. wiss. Bot. 47 (1910)

Barth, R.: Die geotropischen Wachstumskrümmungen der Knoten. Diss. Leipzig 1894

Benecke, W.: Ein Beitrag zur mineralischen Nahrung der Pflanzen. Ber. d. Deutsch. Bot. Ges. 12 (1894)

-: Die zur Ernährung der Schimmelpilze notwendigen Metalle. Jahrb. f. wiss. Bot. 28 (1895)

-: Mechanismus und Biologie des Zerfalls der Konjugatenfäden in die einzelnen Zellen. Jahrb. f. wiss. Bot. 32 (1898)

Berthold, E.: Zur Kenntnis des Verhaltens von Bakterien im Gewebe der Pflanzen. Jahrb. f. wiss. bot. 57 (1917)

Birch-Hirschfeld, L.: Untersuchungen über die Ausbreitungsgeschwindigkeit gelöster Stoffe in der Pflanze. Jahrb. f. wiss. Bot. 59 (1920)

Bolte, E.: Über die Wirkung von Licht und Kohlensäure auf die Beweglichkeit grüner und farbloser Schwärmzellen. Jahrb. f. wiss. Bot. 59 (1920)

Boysen-Jensen, P. (Kopenhagen): La transmission de d'irritation phototropique dans l'Avena. Acad. roy. de Danemark Bull. 1911

-: Über die Leitung des phototropischen Reizes in der Avenakoleoptile. Ber. d. Deutsch. Bot. Ges. 31 (1913)

Brenner, W. (Helsingfors): Züchtungsversuche einiger in Schlamm lebender Bakterien auf selenhaltigem Närboden. Jahrb. f. wiss. Bot. 57 (1917)

Bruck, W.F.: Untersuchungen über den Einfluß von Außenbedingungen auf die Orientierung der Seitenwurzel. Diss. Leipzig 1904. — Zeitschr. f. allg. Physiol. 1904

Brunschorst, J. (Norwegen): Über Wurzelanschwellungen von Alnus und den Elaeagnaceen. Unters. aus dem Botan. Inst. Tübingen. II (1886)

Brunn, J.: Untersuchungen über Stoßreizbarkeit. Diss. Leipzig 1908. — Beitr. zur Biologie d. Pflanzen 9 (1908)

Bücher, H.: Anatomische Veränderungen bei gewaltsamer Krümmung und geotropischer Induktion. Diss. Leipzig 1906. — Jahrb. f. wiss. Bot. 43 (1906)

Bücher, E.: Zuwachsgrößen und Wachstumsgeschwindigkeiten bei Pflansen. Diss. Leipzig 1901

Buller, R. (England): Die Wirkung von Bakterien auf tote Zellen. Diss. Leipzig 1899

Burkhardt, W.: Die Lebensdauer der Pflanzenhaare, ein Beitrag zur Biologie dieser Organe. Diss. Leipzig 1912

Butkewitsch, W. (Rußland): Umwandlung der Eiweißstoffe durch die niederen Pilze im Zusammenhang mit einigen Bedingungen ihrer Entwicklung. Jahrb. f. wiss. Bot. 38 (1903)

Campbell, D. (USA): The staining of living nuclei. Unters. aus dem Botan. Inst. Tübingen II (1888)
Celakovsky, L. (Prag): Über die Aufnahme lebender und toter verdaulicher Körper in die Plasmodien von Myxomyceten. Flora 75 (Erg. band) (1897)
Chapin, P. (USA): Einfluß der Kohlensäure auf das Wachstum. Diss. Leipzig 1902. — Flora 91 (1902)
Chudiakow, N. von (Kiew): Beiträge zur Kenntnis der intramolekularen Atmung. Diss. Leipzig 1894. — Landw. Jahrb. (1894)
-: Untersuchungen über die alkoholische Gährung. Landw. Jahrb. (1894)
Clark (England): Über den Einfluß niederer Sauerstoffpressung auf die Bewegungen des Protoplasmas. Ber. d. Deutsch. Bot. Ges. 6 (1888)
Copeland, E.B. (USA): Einfluß von Licht und Temperatur auf den Turgor. Diss. Halle 1896
Correns, C.: Über die Abhängigkeit der Reizerscheinungen höherer Pflanzen von der Gegenwart freien Sauerstoffs. Flora 75 (1892)
Czapek, F. (Prag): Untersuchungen über Geotropismus. Jahrb. f. wiss. Bot. 27 (1895)
Demoor, J. (Belgien): Contribution à l'étude de la physiologie de la cellule. Archives de Biologie 13 (1894)
Derschau, M. von: Einfluß von Kontakt und Zug auf rankende Blattstiele. Diss. Leipzig 1893
Diakonow, N.W. (Rußland): Intramolekulare Atmung. Ber. d. Deutsch. Bot. Ges. 4 (1886) (Vorl. Mitteilung der später anderweitig erschienenen Abhandlungen)
Dietz, S. (Budapest): Beiträge zur Kenntnis der Substratrichtung der Pflanzen. Unters. aus dem Botan. Inst. Tübingen II (1888)
Dorn, O.: Beiträge zur Kenntnis von der Durchbohrung pflanzlicher Membranen durch Pilzhyphen. Diss. Leipzig 1914

Dude, M.: Über den Einfluß des Sauerstoffentzugs auf pflanzliche Organismen. Diss. Bern 1903. — Flora 92 (1903)

Duggar, M. (USA): Physiological studies with reference to the germination of certain fungous spores. Botan. Gazette 31 (1901)

Ericksson, J. (Schweden): Über Wärmebildung durch intramolekulare Atmung der Pflanzen. Unters. aus dem Botan. Inst. Tübingen, I (1881)

Eschenhagen, F.: Über den Einfluß von Lösungen verschiedener Konzentrationen auf das Wachstum von Schimmelpilzen. Diss. Leipzig 1889

Ewart, A. (England): On assimilatory inhibition in chlorophyllous plants. Diss. Leipzig 1896. — Journ. of the Linnean Society 31 (1896)

-: On the evolution of oxygen from coloured bacteria. Journ. of the Linnean Society 33 (1897)

Ficker, J.: Studien über die Dauer des Orientierungsvermögens der Laubblätter. Diss. Leipzig 1911

Fischer, A.: Einfluß der Schwerkraft auf die Schlafbewegungen der Blätter. Botan. Ztg. (1890), Nr. 42-44

-: Glykose als Reservestoff der Laubhölzer. Botan. Ztg. (1888), Nr. 26

Fitting, H.: Untersuchungen über den Haptotropismus der Ranken. (Vorl. Miteil.). Ber. d. Deutsch. Bot. Ges. 20 (1902)

-: Untersuchungen über den Haptotropismus der Ranken. Jahrb. f. wiss. Bot. 38 (1903)

-: Weitere Untersuchungen zur Physiologie der Ranken nebst einigen neuen Versuchen über die Reizwirkung bei Mimosen. Jahrb. f. wiss. Bot. 39 (1904)

Freundlich, H.: Untersuchungen über die Entwicklung und Regeneration der Gefäßbündel in Kotyledonen und Laubblättern. Diss. Leipzig 1909. — Jahrb. f. wiss. Bot. 46 (1909)

Fritzsche, A.: Untersuchungen über die Lebensdauer und das Absterben der Elemente des Holzkörpers. Diss. Leipzig 1910

Fritzsche, K.: Über die Beeinflussung der Circumnutation durch verschiedene Faktoren. Diss. Leipzig 1899

Gertz, O. (Schweden): Fysiologiska undersökningar öfver slägtet Cuscuta. Botaniska Notiser (1910)

Göbel, J.K.: Über die Durchlässigkeit der Kuticula. Diss. Leipzig 1903

Götze, H.: Hemmung und Richtungsänderung begonnener Differenzierungsprozesse bei Phycomyceten. Jahrb. f. wiss. bot. 58 (1919)

Gräntz, F.: Über den Einfluß des Lichtes auf die Entwicklung einiger Pilze. Diss. Leipzig 1898

Guttenberg, H. von (Triest): Über das Zusammenwirken von Geotropismus und Heliotropismus und die tropistische Empfindlichkeit in reiner und unreiner Luft. Jahrb. f. wiss. Bot. 47 (1910)

Haacke, O. (Erythrea): Über die Ursachen elektrischer Ströme in Pflanzen. Diss. Leipzig 1892. — Flora 75 (1892)

Hahmann, C.: Über Wachstumsstörungen bei Schimmelpilzen durch verschiedene Einflüsse. Diss. Leipzig 1913

Hallbauer, W.: Über den Einfluß allseitiger mechanischer Hemmung durch einen Gipsverband auf die Wachstumszone und die innere Differenzierung der Pflanzen. Diss. Leipzig 1909

Hansgirg (Prag): Phytodynamische Untersuchungen. Prag 1891

Hansteen, B. (Norwegen): Über die Ursachen der Entleerung der Reservestoffe aus Samen. Flora 70 (1894 Ergänzungsband)

Harder, R.: Über den autotropischen Ausgleich mechanisch aufgezwungener Krümmungen des Sprosses. Ber. d. Deutsch. Bot. Ges. 32 (1914)

Hartmann, F.: Beiträge zur Kenntnis der Festigkeits- und Dehnbarkeitzverhältnisse bei Pflanzensprossen. Diss. Leipzig 1913

Hassak, C.: Über das Verhältnis von Pflanzen zu Bikarbonaten und über Kalkinkrustation. Unters. aus dem Botan. Inst. Tübingen II (1888)

Haupt, H.: Zur Sekretionsmechanik der extrafloralen Nektarien. Diss. Leipzig 1900. — Flora 90 (1902)

Hauptfleisch, P.: Untersuchungen über die Strömung des Protoplasmas in behäuteten Zellen. Diss. Leipzig 1892. — Jahrb. f. wiss. Bot. 24 (1892)

Heald de Forest, F. (USA): Gametophytic regeneration as exhibited by mosses and conditions for the germination of cryptogam spores. Diss. Leipzig 1897

Hegler, R.: Über den Einfluß des mechanischen Zugs auf das Wachstum der Pflanze. Diss. Leipzig 1893. — Beitr. z. Biologie d. Pflanzen 6 (1893)

Heinich, K.: Über die Entspannung des Markes im Gewebeverbande und sein Wachstum im isolierten Zustand. Diss. Leipzig 1908. — Jahrb. f. wiss. Bot. 46 (1908)

Heller, A.: Über die Wirkung ätherischer Öle und einiger verwandter Körper auf die Pflanze. Diss. Leipzig 1903. — Flora 93 (1904)

Hering, F.: Über Wachstumskorrelationen bei mechanisch gehemmtem Wachstum. Diss. Leipzig 1896. — Jahrb. f. wiss. Bot. 29 (1896)

Hering, G.: Untersuchungen über das Wachstum invers gestellter Pflanzenorgane. Diss. Leipzig 1904. — Jahrb. f. wiss. Bot. 40 (1904)

Hilbrig, J.: Über den Einfluß supramaximaler Temperatur auf das Wachstum der Pflanzen. Diss. Leipzig 1900

Hilburg, C.: Über Turgescenzänderungen in den Zellen der Bewegungsgelenke. Unters. aus dem Botan. Inst. Tübomgem. I (1881)

Hosseus, K.: Beeinflussung der autonomen Variations-bewegungen durch äußere Faktoren. Diss. Leipzig 1903

Hryniewiecki, B. (Dorpat): Untersuchungen über den Rheotropismus der Wurzeln. Schriften der Naturf. Gesellsch. d. Univ. Jerjeff (Dorpat) (1908), (Russisch mit deutscher Zusammenfassung)

Irmscher, E.: Über die Resistenz der Laubmoose gegen Austrocknung und Kälte. Diss. Leipzig 1912. — Jahrb. f. wiss. Bot. 50 (1912)

Iwanoff, L. (Moskau): Das Auftreten und Schwinden der Phosphorverbindungen in der Pflanze. Jahrb. f. wiss. Bot. 36 (1901)

Jentys, S. (Dablany b. Lemberg): Über den Einfluß hoher Sauerstoffpressungen auf das Wachstum der Pflanzen. Unters. aus dem Botan. Inst. Tübingen II (1881)

Johannsen, W. (Kopenhagen): Über den Einfluß hoher Stauerstoffspannung auf die Kohlensäureausscheidung einiger Keimpflanzen. Unters. aus dem Botan. Inst. Tübingen I (1885)

Josing, E.: Die Einfluß der Außenbedingungen auf die Abhängigkeit der Protoplasmaströmung vom Licht. Diss. Leipzig 1901. — Jahrb. f. wiss. bot. 36 (1901)

Juel, O.H. (Schweden): Untersuchungen über den Rheotropismus der Wurzeln. Jahrb. f. wiss. Bot. 34 (1900)

Kaiser, J.F.: Vergleichende Untersuchungen über den Einfluß von Abtrennungen und Verwundungen auf die geotropische Reaktion von Pflanzenorganen. Diss. Leipzig 1907

Katz, J.: Die regulatorische Bildung von Diatase durch Pilze. Jahrb. f. wiss. Bot. 31 (1898)

Keller, I. (USA): Protoplasmaströmung im Pflanzenreich. Diss. Zürich 1890

Kerstan, K.: Über den Einfluß des geotropischen und heliotropischen Reizes auf den Turgordruck in den Geweben. Diss. Leipzig 1907. — Beitr. z. Biologie d. Pflanzen 9 (1907)

Klebs, G.: Über die Organisation einiger Flagellaten-Gruppen und ihre Beziehungen zu Algen und Infusorien. Unters. aus dem Botan. Inst. Tübingen I (1883)

-: Beiträge zur Morphologie und Biologie der Keimung. Unters. aus dem Botan. Inst. Tübingen I (1885)

-: Über die Organisation der Gallerte bei einigen Algen und Flagellaten. Unters. aus dem Botan. Inst. Tübingen II (1886)

-: Beiträge zur Physiologie der Pflanzenzelle. Unters. aus dem Botan. Inst. Tübingen II (1888)

Klemm, P.: Beitrag zur Erforschung der Aggregationsvorgänge in lebenden Pflanzenzellen. Flora 75 (1892)

-: Über die Aggregationsvorgänge in Crassulaceenzellen. Ber. d. Deutsch. Bot. Ges. 10 (1892)

-: Desorganisationserscheinungen der Zelle. Jahrb. f. wiss. bot. 24 (1895)

Klercker, J.E.F. af (Schweden): Studien über Gerbstoffvakuolen. Diss. 1888. — Bihang till K. Svenska Vet. Akad. Handlingar 13 Afd. III No. 8

Kurzwelly, W.: Über die Widerstandsfähigkeit trockener pflanzlicher Organismen gegen giftige Stoffe. Diss. Leipzig 1903. — Jahrb. f. wiss. Bot. 38 (1903)

Kylin, H. (Schweden): Über Enzymbildung und Enzymregulation bei einigen Schimmelpilzen. Jahrb. f. wiss. Bot. 53 (1914)

Lange, T.: Beiträge zur Kenntnis der Entwicklung der Gefäße und Tracheiden. Diss. Leipzig 1891. — Flora 74 (1891)

Lehmann, E.: Zur Kenntnis des anaeroben Wachstums höherer Pflanzen. Jahrb. f. wiss. Bot. 49 (1911)

Leonhardt, W.: Über das Durchbrechen und das Verhalten von Sprossen bei zu hoher oder viel Widerstand bietender Erdbedeckung. Diss. Leipzig 1915. — Jahrb. f. wiss. Bot. 55 (1915)

Lepeschkin, W. (Moskau): Bedeutung der Wasser absondernden Organe für die Pflanzen. Flora 90 (1902)

Lieske, R.: Beiträge zur Kenntnis der Physiologie von Spirophyllum ferrugineum Ellis, einem typischen Eisenbakterium. Diss. Leipzig 1911. — Jahrb. f. wiss. Bot. 49 (1911)

-: Untersuchungen über die Physiologie eisenspeichernder Hyphomyceten. Jahrb. f. wiss. Bot. 50 (1912)

-: Untersuchungen über die Physiologie denitrifizierender Schwefelbakterien. Sitzungsber. d. Heidelberger Akad. d. Wiss., Biolog. Wissensch. 1912, 6. Abhandl.

Lind, K.: Über das Eindringen von Pilzen in Kalkgesteine und Knochen. Diss. Leipzig 1899. — Jahrb. f. wiss. Bot. 32 (1899)

Lindner, J.: Über den Einfluß günstiger Temperaturen auf gefrorene Schimmelpilze. (Zur Kenntnis der Kälteresistenz von Aspergillus niger.) Diss. Leipzig 1915. — Jahrb. f. wiss. bot. 55 (1915)

Kniep, H.: Untersuchungen über die Chemotaxis der Bakterien. Jahrb. f. wiss. Bot. 43 (1906)

Köhler, P.: Beiträge zur Kenntnis der Reproduktions- und Regenerationsvorgänge bei Pilzen und der Bedingungen des Absterbens mycelialer Zellen von Aspergillus niger. Diss. Leipzig 1907. — Flora 97 (1907)

Köhler, R.: Über die plastischen und anatomischen Veränderungen bei Keimwurzeln und Luftwurzeln, hervorgerufen durch partielle mechanische Hemmungen. Diss. Leipzig 1902

Koernicke, M.: Über die Wirkung von Röntgenstrahlen auf die Keimung und das Wachstum. Ber. d. Deutsch. Bot. Ges. 22 (1904)

Kosanin, N. (Serbien): Über den Einfluß von Temperatur und Ätherdampf auf die Lage der Laubblätter. Diss. Leipzig 1905

Kosaroff, P. (Rußland): Einfluß verschiedener äußerer Faktoren auf die Wasseraufnahme der Pflanzen. Diss. Leipzig 1897

Kosinski, I. (Bulgarien): Die Atmung bei Hungerzuständen und unter Einwirkung von mechanischen und chemischen Reizmitteln bei Aspergillus niger. Diss. Leipzig 1901. — Jahrb. f. wiss. Bot. 37 (1902)

Kretzschmar, P.: Über Entstehung und Ausbreitung der Protoplasmaströmung infolge von Wundreiz. Diss. Leipzig 1903. — Jahrb. f. wiss. Bot. 39 (1903)

Krezemieniewski, S. (Krakau): Ein Beitrag zur Kenntnis der phototaktischen Bewegungen. Anz. d. Akad. d. Wiss. zu Krakau, Abt. II (1909), II. Semester

Kunstmann, H.: Über das Verhältnis zwischen Pilzernte und verbrauchter Nahrung. Diss. Leipzig 1895

Liro, I. (Helsingfors): Über die photochemische Chlorophyllbildung bei den Phanerogamen. Annales Acad. scientiarum Fennicae Ser. A, tom. I (1908)

Lundegardh. H. (Schweden): Einige Bedingungen der Bildung und Auflösung der Stärke. Jahrb. f. wiss. bot. 53 (1914)

Luxburg, H. Graf von: Untersuchungen über den Wachstumsverlauf bei der geotropischen Bewegung. Diss. Leipzig 1905. — Jahrb. f. wiss. Bot. 41 (1905)

Mac Dougal (USA): The mechanism of movement and transmission of impulses in Mimosa and other sensitive plants. Botan. Gaz. 22 (1896)

McKenney, R. (USA): Observations on the conditions of light production in luminous bacteria. Diss. Basel 1902. — Proceedings of the Biol. Soc. of Washington 15 (1902)

Mann, B.: Untersuchungen über die Zellhautbildung um plasmolysierte Protoplasten. Diss. Leipzig 1906

Mayenburg, O. von: Lösungskonzentration und Turgorregulation bei den Schimmelpilzen. Diss. Leipzig 1901. — Jahrb. f. wiss. Bot. 36 (1901)

Meischke, P.: Über die Arbeitsleistung der Pflanzen bei der geotropischen Krümmung. Diss. Leipzig 1898. — Jahrb. f. wiss. Bot. 33 (1899)

Meissner, C.: Akkommodationsfähigkeit einiger Schimmelpilze. Diss. Leipzig 1902

Meurer, R.: Über die regulatorische Aufnahme anorganischer Stoffe durch die Wurzeln von Beta vulgaris und Daucus Carota. Diss. Leipzig 1909. — Jahrb. f. wiss. Bot. 46 (1909)

Meyer, J.: Die Crataegomespili von Bronvaux. Diss. Leipzig 1915. — Zeitschr. f. induktive Abst. u. Vererbungslehre 13 (1915)

Miehe, H.: Über korrelative Beeinflussung des Geotropismus einiger Gelenkpflanzen. Jahrb. f. wiss. Bot. 37 (1902)

Miyoshi, M. (Japan): Über den Chemotropismus der Pilze. Botan. Ztg. 1894

-: Über Reizbewegungen der Pollenschläuche. Flora 78 (1894)

-: Die Durchbohrung von Membranen durch Pilzfäden. Jahrb. f. wiss. Bot. 28 (1895)

Mogk, W.: Untersuchungen über Korrelationen von Knospen und Sprossen. Diss. Leipzig 1913. — Archiv f. Entwicklungsmechanik 38 (1914)

Moisescu, N. (Rumänien): Kleine Mitteilung über die Anwendung des horizontalen Mikroskopes zur Bestimmung der Reaktionszeit. Ber. d. Deutsch. Bot. Ges. 23 (1905)

Morgenstern, R.: Über den mechanischen Ausgleich der durch Verhinderung der geotropischen Krümmung in den Pflanzen entstandenen Spannungen. Diss. Leipzig 1913. — Beiträge z. Biologie der Pflanzen 12 (1913)

Mottier, D.M. (USA): The effect of centrifugal force upon the cell. Ann. of Botany 13 (1899)

Müller, C. (Dobrowitz, Österreich): Über die Entstehung von Kalkoxalatkristallen in pflanzlichen Zellmembranen. Diss. Leipzig 1890

Müller, F.: Untersuchungen über die chemotaktische Reizbarkeit der Zoosporen von Chytridiaceen und Saprolegniaceen. Diss. Leipzig 1911. — Jahrb. f. wiss. Bot. 49 (1911)

Müller, G.: Beiträge zur Keimungsphysiologie. Diss. Leipzig 1915. — Jahrb. f. wiss. Bot. 54 (1914)

Nathansohn, A. (Österreich): Beiträge zur Kenntnis des Wachstums der trachealen Elemente. Jahrb. f. wiss. Bot. 32 (1898)

-: Physiologische Untersuchungen über amitotische Kernteilung. Diss. Leipzig 1900. — Jahrb. f. wiss. Bot. 35 (1900)

-: (zusammen mit Pringsheim, E.): Über die Summation intermittierender Lichtreize. Jahrb. f. wiss. Bot. 45 (1908)

Nedokutschaeff, N. (Rußland): Über die Speicherung der Nitrate in den Pflanzen. (Vorl. Mitt.) Ber. d. Deutsch. Bot. Ges. 21 (1903)

Neubert, L.: Geotrophismus und Kamptotrophismus bei Blattstielen. Diss. Leipzig 1911. — Beitr. z. Biologie d. Pflanzen 10 (1911)

Neubert, R.O.: Untersuchungen über die Nutationskrümmungen des Keimblattes von Allium. Diss. Leipzig 1903. — Jahrb. f. wiss. Bot. 38 (1903)

Newcombe, F.C. (USA): The effect of mechanical resistance on the growth of plant tissues. Diss. Leipzig 1894

-: The influence of mechanical resistance on the development and life-period of cells. Botan. Gazette 19 (1894)

-: The cause and condition of lysigenous cavity-formation. Ann. of Botany 8 (1894)

Nikitinsky, J. (Moskau): Über die Beeinflussung einiger Pilze durch ihre Stoffwechselprodukte. Jahrb. f. wiss. Bot. 40 (1904)

Niklewski, B.S.: Untersuchungen über die Umwandlung einiger stickstoffreicher Reservestoffe während der Winterperiode der Bäume. Diss. Leipzig

-: Über die Wasserstoffoxydation durch Mikroorganismen. Jahrb. f. wiss. Bot. 48 (1910)

Popovici, A.P. (Rumänien): Der Einfluß der Vegetationsbedingungen auf die Länge der wachsenden Zone. Botan. Centralbl. 81 (1900)

Porodko, T. (Rußland): Studien über den Einfluß der Sauerstoffspannung auf pflanzliche Mikroorganismen. Jahrb. f. wiss. Bot. 41 (1905)

-: Nimmt die ausgewachsene Region des orthotropen Stengels an der geotropischen Krümmung teil? Ber. d. Deutsch. Bot. Ges. 26 a (1908)

Pringsheim, E.: Wasserbewegung und Turgorregulation in welkenden Pflanzen. Diss. Leipzig 1906. — Jahrb. f. wiss. Bot. 43 (1906)

- und Nathanson, A.: Siehe diesen

Pulst, K.: Die Widerstandsfähigkeit einiger Schimmelpilze gegen Metallgifte. Diss. Leipzig 1902. — Jahrb. f. wiss. Bot. 37 (1902)

Puriewitsch, K. (Kiew): Über selbsttätige Entleerung der Reservestoffbehälter. (Vorl. Mitteilung) Ber. d. Deutsch. Bot. Ges. 14 (1896)

-: Physiologische Untersuchungen über die Entleerung der Reservestoffbehälter. Jahrb. f. wiss. Bot. 31 (1898)

Rabe, F.: Über die Austrocknungsfähigkeit gekeimter Samel und Sporen. Diss. Leipzig 1905. — Flora 95 (Ergänzungsband, 1905)

Renner, O.: Experimentelle Beiträge zur Wasserversorgung. Flora 103 (1911)

Richards, H.M. (USA): The respiration of wounded plants. Ann. of botany 10 (1896)

-: Die Beeinflussung des Wachstums einiger Pilze durch chemische Reize. Jahrb. f. wiss. Bot. 30 (1897)

-: The evolution of heat by wounded plants. Ann. of botany 11 (1897)

Noack, K.: Beiträge zur Biologie der thermophilen Organismen. Diss. Leipzig 1913. — Jahrb. f. wiss. Bot. 51 (1813)

Nordhausen, M.: Beiträge zur Biologie parasitärer Pilze. Jahrb. f. wiss. Bot. 33 (1899)

Ohno, N. (Japan): Über das Abklingen von geotropischen und heliotropischen Reizvorgängen. Jahrb. f. wiss. Bot. 45 (1908)

Oliver, F.W. (England): Fortleitung des Reizes bei Narben. Ber. d. Deutsch. Bot. Ges. (1887)

Paál, A. (Budapest): Über phototropische Reizleitungen. (Vorl. Mitt.) Ber. d. Deutsch. Bot. Ges. 32 (1914)

-: Über phototropische Reizleitung. Jahrb. f. wiss. Bot. 58 (1919)

Pantanelli, E. (Italien): Zur Kenntnis der Turgorregulation bei Schimmelpilzen. Jahrb. f. wiss. Bot. 40 (1904)

Peirce, G.J. (USA): A contribution to the physiology of the genus Cuscuta. Diss. Leipzig 1894. — Ann. of Botany 8 (1894)

-: Das Eindringen von Wurzeln in lebendige Gewebe. Botan. Ztg. 52 (1894)

Pfundt, M.: Der Einfluß der Luftfeuchtigkeit auf die Lebensdauer des Blütenstaubes. Diss. Leipzig 1909. — Jahrb. f. wiss. Bot. 47 (1909)

Pollock, J.B. (USA): The effect of shock on longitudinal growth of plant organs. Science N.S., 13 (1901)

Richter, J.: Über Reaktionen der Characeen auf äußere Einflüsse. Diss. Leipzig 1894. — Flora 78 (1894)

Ritter, G. (Moskau): Die Abhängigkeit der Plasmaströmung und der Geißelbewegung vom freien Sauerstoff. Flora 86 (1899)

Rothert, W. (Kasan): Über die Fortpflanzung des heliotropischen Reizes. Ber. d. Deutsch. Bot. Ges. 10 (1892)

-: Über Heliotropismus. Beitr. z. Biologie der Pflanzen 7 (1896)

-: Beobachtungen und Betrachtungen über taktische Reizerscheinungen. Flora 88 (1901)

-: Zur Terminologie der taktischen Reizerscheinungen. Botan. Ztg. 60 (1902)

-: Über die Wirkung des Äthers und Chloroforms auf die Reizbewegungen der Mikroorganismen. Jahrb. f. wiss. Bot. 39 (1904)

Rysselberghe, F. van (Belgien): Influence de la température sur la perméabilité du protoplasma vivant. Bullet. d l'Academie royale de Belgique (Classe des sciences) No. 3 (1901)

Schröder, G.: Über die Austrocknungsfähigkeit der Pflanzen. Unters. aus dem Botan. Inst. Tübingen II (1886)

Schröter, A.: Über Protoplasmaströmung bei Mucorineen. Diss. Leipzig 1905. — Flora 95 (Ergänzungsband, 1905)

Schtscherback, J. (Odessa): Die geotropische Reaktion in gespaltenen Stengeln. Beihefte z. Botan. Centralbl. 251. Abt. (1910)

Schubert, W.: Über die Resistenz exsiccatortrockener pflanzlicher Organismen gegen Alkohol und Chloroform bei höheren Temperaturen. Diss. Leipzig 1909. — Flora 100 (1910)

Schüller, F.: Über die Umwandlung der Kohlehydrate während der Jahresperiode in den Halbsträuchern und perennierenden Kräutern. Diss. Leipzig 1898

Schuster, G.: Über den Einfluß der Sauerstoffpressung auf die Protoplasmaströmung. Diss. Leipzig 1913

Schütze, J.: Die Beeinflussung des Wachstums durch den Turgeszenzzustand. Diss. Leipzig 1908

Schütze, R.: Über das geotropische Verhalten des Hypokotyls und des Kotyledons. Diss. Leipzig 1910. — Jahrb. f. wiss. Bot. 48 (1910)

Schwarz, F. (Österreich): Die Wurzelhaare der Pflanzen. Unters. aus dem Botan. Inst. Tübingen I (1884)

-: Zur Kritik der Methode des Gasblasenzählens an submersen Wasserpflanzen. Unters. aus dem Botan. Inst. Tübingen I (1881)

-: Der Einfluß der Schwerkraft auf das Längenwachstum der Pflanzen. Unters. aus dem Botan. Inst. Tübingen I (1881)

Senn, G. (Schweiz): Die Gestalts- und Lageveränderungen der Pflanzenchromatophoren. Leipzig 1908

Shibata, K. (Japan): Untersuchungen über lockere Bindung von Sauerstoff in gewissen farbstoffbildenden Bakterien und Pilzen. Jahrb. f. wiss. Bot. 51 (1912)

Simon, S.: Untersuchungen über das Verhalten einiger Wachstumsfunktionen sowie die Atmungsfähigkeit der Laubhölzer während der Ruheperiode. Jahrb. f. wiss. Bot. 38 (1903)

-: Untersuchungen über die Regeneration der Wurzelspitze. Diss. Leipzig 1904. — Jahrb. f. wiss. Bot. 40 (1904)

-: Experimentelle Untersuchungen über die Differenzierungsvorgänge im Callusgewebe von Holzgewächsen. Jahrb. f. wiss. Bot. 45 (1908)

Spalding, M.V. (USA): The traumatropic curvature of roots. Diss. Leipzig 1894. — Ann. of Botany 8 (1894)

Sperlich, A. (Österreich): Über die Krümmungsursachen bei Keimstengeln und beim Monokotylenkeimblatte nebst Bemerkungen über den Phototropismus der positiv geotropischen Zonen des Hypokotyls und über das Stemmorgan bei Cucurbitaceen. Jahrb. f. wiss. Bot. 50 (1912)

Stange, B.: Über chemotaktische Reizbewegungen. I. Die Zoosporen der Saprolegniaceen. 2. Die Myxamöben der Myxomyceten. Botan. Ztg. (1890), Nr. 7-11

-: Beziehungen zwischen Substratkonzentration, Turgor und Wachstum bei einigen phanerogamen Pflanzen. Diss. Leipzig 1892. — Botan. Ztg. (1892), Nr. 16-27

Steyer, K.: Reizkrümmungen bei Phycomyces nitens. Diss. Leipzig 1901

Stark, P.: Untersuchungen über Kontaktreizbarkeit. Ber. d. Deutsch. Bot. Ges. 33 (1915)

-: Experimentelle Untersuchungen über das Wesen und die Verbreitung der Kontaktreizbarkeit. Jahrb. f. wiss. Bot. 57 (1917)

Stich, C.: Atmung der Pflanzen bei verminderter Sauerstoffspannung und bei Verletzungen. Diss. Leipzig 1890. — Flora 74 (1891)

Thiele, R.: Die Temperaturgrenze der Schimmelpilze in verschiedenen Nährlösungen. Diss. Leipzig 1896

Tittmann, H.: Physiologische Untersuchungen über Kallusbildung an Stecklingen holziger Gewächse. Jahrb. f. wiss. Bot. 27 (1894)

-: Beobachtungen über Bildung und Regeneration des Periderms der Epidermis, des Wachsüberzuges und der Kutikula einiger Gewächse. Diss. Leipzig 1897. — Jahrb. f. wiss. Bot. 30 (1897)

Townsend, Ch. (USA): Der Einfluß des Zellkerns auf die Bildung der Zellhaut. Diss. Leipzig 1897. — Jahrb. f. wiss. Bot. 30 (1897)

-: The correlation of growth under the influence of injuries. Ann. of Botany 11 (1897)

Trebitz, E.: Beiträge zur Kenntnis der Ergrünungsbedingungen der Pflanzen. Diss. Leipzig 1905

Treboux, O.: Einige stoffliche Einflüsse auf die Kohlensäureassimilation bei submersen Pflanzen. Diss. Leipzig 1903. — Flora 92 (1903)

True, R.H. (USA): On the influence of sudden changes of turgor and of temperature on growth. Diss. Leipzig 1895. — Ann. of Botany 9 (1895)

Trülzsch, O.: Über die Ursachen der Dorsiventralität der Sprosse von Ficus pumila und einiger anderer Pflanzen. Diss. Leipzig 1914. — Jahrb. f. wiss. Bot. 54 (1914)

Trzebinski, J. (Warschau): Über den Einfluß verschiedener Reize auf das Wachstum von Phycomyces nitens. Anz. d. Akad. d. Wiss. zu Krakau, 1902

Voegler, C.: Beiträge zur Kenntnis der Reizerscheinungen an Samenfäden der Farne. Diss. Leipzig 1891. — Botan. Ztg. (1891)

Wacker, J. (Holland): Die Beeinflussung des Wachstums der Wurzeln durch das umgebende Medium. Diss. Leipzig 1898. — Jahrb. f. wiss. Bot. 32 (1898)

Wächter, W.: Untersuchungen über den Austritt von Zucker aus den Zellen der Speicherorgane von Allium Cepa und Beta vulgaris. Jahrb. f. wiss. Bot. 41 (1905)

Warburg, O.: Über die Bedeutung der organischen Säuren für den Lebensprozeß der Pflanzen (speziell der sog. Fettpflanzen). Unters. aus dem Botan. Inst. Tübingen II (1886)

Wehmer, C.: Entstehung und physiologische Bedeutung der Oxalsäure im Stoffwechsel einiger Pilze. Botan. Ztg. (1891), Nr. 15-38

-: Zur Zersetzung der Oxalsäure durch Licht- und Stoffwechselwirkung. Ber. d. Deutsch. Bot. Ges. 9 (1891)

-: Über den Einfluß der Temperatur auf die Entstehung freier Oxalsäure in Kulturen von Aspergillus niger. Ber. d. Deutsch. Bot. Ges. 9 (1891)

Weinert, J.: Untersuchungen über Wachstum und tropistische Bewegungserscheinungen der Rhizoiden thallöser Lebermoose. Diss. Leipzig 1909. — Botan. Ztg. 67 (1909)

Wiedersheim, W. (Italien): Studien über photonastische und thermonastische Bewegungen. Jahrb. f. wiss. Bot. 40 (1904)

Wieler, A.: Die Beeinflussung des Wachsens durch verminderte Partiärpressung des Sauerstoffs. Unters. aus dem Botan. Inst. Tübingen I (1883)

- Das Bluten der Pflanzen. Beitr. z. Biologie der Pflanzen 6 (1893)
- Die Jahresperiode des Blutens. Tharandter forstl. Jahrbuch 43 (1893)

Wilson, W. (USA): The cause of the excretion of water on the surface of nectaries. Unters. aus den Botan. Inst. Tübingen I (1881)

Winkler, A.: Über den Einfluß der Außenbedingungen auf die Kälteresistenz ausdauernder Gewächse. Diss. Leipzig 1913. — Jahrb. f. wiss. Bot. 52 (1913)

Winkler, E.: Krümmungsbewegungen von Spirogyra. Diss. Leipzig 1902

Winkler, H.: Untersuchungen über die Stärkebildung in den verschiedenartigen Chromatophoren. Diss. Leipzig 1898. — Jahrb. f. wiss. Bot. 32 (1898)

Wohllebe, H.: Untersuchungen über die Ausscheidung von diastatischen und proteolytischen Enzymen bei Samen und Wurzeln. Diss. Leipzig 1911

Zehl, B.: Die Beeinflussung der Giftwirkung durch die Temperatur, sowie durch das Zusammengreifen von zwei Giften. Diss. Leipzig 1907. — Zeitschrift f. allgem. Physiologie 8 (1908)

Zinsser, O.: Über das Verhalten von Bakterien, insbesondere von Knöllchenbakterien in lebenden pflanzlichen Geweben. Diss. Leipzig 1897. — Jahrb. f. wiss. Bot. 30 (1897)

VISITING SCHOLARS

This is a list of visiting scholars from outside Germany who came to work with Pfeffer. These names are in addition to those which appear in the preceding list of publications by Pfeffer's collaborators.

Akermann, A. (Sweden) 1914-15
Massart, J. (Belgium) 1892
Artari, A. (Moscow) 1899
Maurizio, A. (Lemberg) 1909-10
Barladean, A. (Bessarabia) 1910-12
Medisch, M. (Kharkov) 1910-11
Faber, F.v. (Amsterdam) 1903
Peklo, J. (Prague) 1909-10
Fehlner (Austria) before 1887
Perekalin, B. (Moscow) 1910
Frankfurt, S. (Wilno) 1896)
Rosenvinge, L.K. (Copenhagen) before 1887
Goodale, G.L. (USA) before 1887
Schröder, R. (Moscow) 1902
Holman, R. (USA) 1912-14
Stone, G.E. (USA) 1890-92
Hume, A. (USA) 1908
Svedelius, N.E. (Sweden) 1912
Issatschenko (Petersburg) 1896)
Swingle, W.J. (USA) 1892
Jensen (Copenhagen) 1892
Szücs, J. (Hungary) 1912-13
Jönsson, B. (Sweden) before 1887
Uhlehla, V. (Moravia) 1912-13
Keeble, F. (England) 1893
Wulff, Th. (Sweden) 1902
Lidforss, B. (Sweden) 1893 and 1906

BIOGRAPHICAL NOTES

Bernard, Claude; 1813-1878
French physiologist, one of the founders of modern, experimental medicine. Published works on the function of the pancreas, on the role of the liver in carbohydrate metabolism, on the function of the vasomotor nerves, and on the control of individual organs by the nervous system. Bernard also recognized the principle of the dynamic equilibrium of the organism. Bernard's achievements were characteristic of the advanced stage of experimental physiology in France in those days. It was only fitting that he was given a state funeral; he was the first French scientist to be honoured in this manner.

Boysen Jensen, Peter; 1883-1959
"Thanks to his initiative - using a sharp mind and delicate soma - plant physiology research became established in Denmark" (D. Müller, in an obituary, *Ber. deutsch. Bot. Ges.*, 74, 1962). The areas in which Boysen Jensen worked included respiration and fermentation, yeast metabolism, hormones, productivity from the point of view of physiology and ecology, and the conversion of substances on the sea bottom. Several of his books were published in Danish and German, and some also appeared in English and Russian.

Clausius, Rudolf Julius Emanuel; 1822-1888
After receiving his doctorate, he taught at the university level in Berlin. Thereafter he held professorships in Zürich, Würzburg and Bonn. He is considered a founder of a theory of mechanical heat. He introduced the term "entropy" and clearly formulated the second law of thermodynamics.

Correns, Carl Erich; 1864-1933

He studied botany in Munich and Graz. In 1891, he changed the focus of his studies because his sight was affected by the excessive use of the microscope. For a short time he went to work with Pfeffer. Thereafter he taught at the universities in Tübingen, Leipzig and Münster. From 1914 onward, he worked at the Institute of Biology (he became the director) of the Kaiser-Wilhelm-Institute [now Max-Planck-Institute] in Berlin. His earlier research covered different areas of botany. In 1900 he became one of the re-discoverers of Mendel's laws; thereafter he concentrated his efforts with great success on genetics.

De Candolle, Augustin Pyrame; 1778-1841

He was born in Switzerland. He studied botany, first in his native land, and then in Paris. He had a close contact as a scientist with Lamarck. Later, he was a Professor of Botany in Geneva. He worked with success in many areas of botany, and was an innovator in some. However, he was still a proponent of vitalism, and he thought that "sensitivity" was a factor that distinguished animals from plants.

De Vries, Hugo; 1848-1935

Dutch botanist. After receiving his doctorate, he worked under Hofmeister. He was a high-school teacher in Amsterdam for several years, but during his vacations he worked under Sachs in Würzburg. De Vries was a botanist of many talents. He is well known for his investigations into the osmotic activity of plant cells and for his research in genetics (he was another re-discoverer of Mendel's law). In addition, he worked with great success in a variety of areas of plant physiology. "He was a powerful thinker" for whom "the visionary idea held primacy over experience... he will continue to live in memory as one of the greatest biologists around the turn of the nineteenth and twentieth centuries." (O. Renner, in *Naturwissenschaften*, 24, (1936), pp. 321-324.)

Driesch, Hans; 1867-1941
He was an expert in developmental physiology with emphasis on zoology. His study of the phenomena of regulatory processes played a major role in a change of direction to philosophy. He eventually became a Professor of Philosophy at the University in Leipzig.

Du Bois-Reymond, Emil; 1818-1896
Professor of Physiology at Berlin University. He published many works on electro-physiology, and on the physiology of nerves and muscles. He was much involved with philosophical questions relating to natural sciences.

Dutrochet, Henri Joaquim; 1776-1847
French medical doctor and physiologist. He is one of the thinkers who, early on, took a strong stand against vitalism. Dutrochet investigated osmosis, and he accomplished much pioneering work in plant physiology. He was the first to interpret the geotropic action of plants as a triggering mechanism.

Ehrlich, Paul; 1854-1915
After completing his medical studies, he worked first in Berlin and then in Frankfurt/Main. He is the founder of chemotherapy, and he was an outstanding immunologist. His discovery of salvarasan made him famous. In 1908, he received the Nobel Prize for Physiology and Medicine. See *Grosse Naturforscher*, Vol. 8, by H. Loewe on Paul Ehrlich.

Goebel, Karl von; 1855-1932.
His first studies were in theology, but he soon changed to botany. His scientific development was shaped to a large

extent by Hofmeister; however, he was also influenced by de Bary and Sachs. Goebel was a professor at the universities in Rostock, Marburg and Munich. Morphology and development were his areas of greatest interest. He was both a writer and an experimenter (Goebel stated: "Morphology is that which cannot yet be explained physiologically."). He compiled many of the results of his own work in *Organigraphie der Pflanzen*, a publication of several volumes. He became widely known through his connection with the founding of the famous new Botanical Garden in Munich. There can be no doubt that he was one of the greatest botanists of his day.

Haberlandt, Gottlieb; 1854-1945

He was born in Imperial Austro-Hungary. He studied and received his doctorate at the University of Vienna. He worked at the universities in Tubingen and Vienna. At the age of twenty-six, he was appointed professor at the University of Graz. Later, he became a professor at the university in Berlin. Haberlandt is the founder of physiological plant anatomy. He tried to determine the significance of the functions relating to detailed anatomical parts (initially he met strong opposition from leading contemporary botanists). In World War II he fled to Silesia from the hail of bombs in Berlin. When the Soviet armies approached he fled from Silesia back to Berlin, where he found his house destroyed by bombs. It proved to be more than a ninety-year old could endure.

Haberlandt wrote an autobiography: *Erinnerungen, Bekenntnisse und Betrachtungen* (Berlin, 1933).

Helmholtz, Hermann von; 1821-1894

He was one of the greatest scientists of his time, both as a physicist and as a biologist. Medicine was his major subject of study, and for a while he was a military doctor.

Thereafter he was a Professor of Physiology at the universities in Königsberg, Bonn and Heidelberg; and then, a Professor of Physics at Berlin University. He was the first president of the *Physikalisch-Technische Reichsanstalt* (Berlin). In 1847, he published his treatise, *Von der Erhaltung der Kraft.* Other publications cover the subjects of acoustics and optics. See *Grosse Naturforscher*, Vol. 5, by H. Ebert on Hermann von Helmholtz.

Hofmeister, Wilhelm; 1824-1877
At the age of fifteen, he apprenticed in a music shop. He taught himself mathematics and sciences, often starting in the morning at five o'clock before going to work. In recognition of his early publications on problems of plant morphology and development, the twenty-six year old Hofmeister was awarded an honorary doctorate by the University of Rostock. He was thirty-nine before he was able to take up botany as a full-time activity. He was appointed to an *Ordinariat* [full professorship] for Botany at the University of Heidelberg. This appointment by the Ministry of the Grand Duchy of Baden was made over the heads of the university faculty. Subsequently, Hofmeister was the *Ordinarius* for Botany at the University of Tübingen. This was a man who had not obtained a high school diploma or followed a university education. His greatest achievement was the discovery of homologies in the alternation of generations of mosses, ferns and seed plants. Eight years after this revelation, when "Darwin's evolutionary teachings appeared, the family connections between the major divisions of the plant world . . . were so clearly apparent that the evolutionary theory only had to confirm what genetic morphology had already demonstrated" (J. Sachs in his book, *Geschichte der Botanik*).

Kniep, Hans; 1881-1930

He studied under Ernest Stahl in Jena, and he worked under Chodat in Geneva, Pfeffer in Leipzig, and Oltmanns (an expert on algae) in Freiburg. He became a *Dozent* [lecturer] at the University of Freiburg, and thereafter he held professorships at the universities in Strassburg, Würzburg and Berlin. He worked in the area of the physiology of stimulation, and in particular, on the development, propagation, and sexuality of fungi and algae.

Liebig, Justus von; 1803-1873

He is best known as the man who introduced artificial fertilizers; he is also the discoverer of Liebig's meat extract and of baking powder. He started his studies under Guy Lussac in Paris; next, he became a professor at the university in Giessen. There, he established the first chemistry institute in Germany. Later, he was a professor at the university in Munich. He put out many publications on biochemical research. He had the correct idea on how plants take up nourishment, but was mistaken on some other matters. Thus, he opposed Pasteur's interpretation of fermentation. He stood very much under the influence of Schelling's "Philosophy of Nature."

Loeb, Jacques; 1859-1924

He was born in Germany. He studied in Germany and worked there as a teaching assistant. From 1891, he lived in the USA, and became a professor of physiology and experimental biology. Loeb's research included work on fertilization in animals, on the physical and chemical factors in the induction of development of unfertilized eggs, on regeneration in plants and animals, and on the physical chemistry of endosperms. He wrote a great deal on general physiology; however, while he achieved valuable results in his experiments, he also tended to draw conclusions which were too sweeping, and which did not do justice to the complexities of the organism. Thus, he also overstated the importance of tropism for the behaviour of animals.

Mayer, Julius Robert; 1814-1878
He was a physician. His discovery of the principle of the conservation of energy was not the result of experimentation and correct conclusions. The starting point was an observation he made during a voyage as a ship's doctor. He noticed that during bloodletting in the tropics, the colour of the blood was lighter than when the procedure was used in Europe. When he realized this, ideas came to him like a "flash of lightning." His original report contained errors of basic physics, and it was not accepted for publication. Later, Mayer himself admitted these mistakes.

Meyerhof, Otto; 1884-1951
He was born in Germany, emigrated to Paris in 1938, and fled to the USA in 1940. Meyerhof was a professor at the University of Kiel, then he worked at the Kaiser Wilhelm Institute in Berlin, and later in Heidelberg. In the USA, he worked at the University of Pennsylvania. In 1922, he shared the Nobel Prize in Medicine and Physiology with A.V. Hill. He was given the award in recognition of his research on muscle metabolism.

Mohl, Hugo von; 1805-1872
He was one of the foremost investigators of the cell in the nineteenth century. He was Professor of Physiology at the University of Bern, and after 1835, he was Professor of Botany at the University of Tübingen. The word "protoplasma" was already used by Purkinje, but von Mohl was the first (in 1846) to use the expression in the

same sense as it is still understood today. Von Mohl was the foremost proponent for the creation of a distinct faculty of mathematics and natural sciences at the University of Tübingen — the first of its kind in Germany. It was formed in 1863 by separating it from the Faculty of Philosophy. The Botanical Institute was built in 1846 while von Mohl held office. It is the same building in which Pfeffer worked, and it functioned as a botanical institute (with certain enlargements) until 1968.

Müller, Johannes; 1801-1858

He was an anatomist and a physiologist. He published research papers on reflex movements and on other physiological questions. He wrote the two volume *Handbuch der Physiologie des Menschen.* See *Grosse Naturforscher,* Vol. 23, by G. Koller on Johannes Müller.

Nägeli, Carl; 1817-1891

He was born in Zürich. In his early thinking he was influenced by Oken. He studied botany under de Candolle in Geneva. Later, he studied philosophy under Hegel in Berlin. Even though he strongly rejected Hegel's thinking, he still showed distinct traces of Oken's and Hegel's thinking. He held professorships in Zürich, Freiburg and Munich. He is credited with a great number of investigations in cytology and development. Several valuable points of departure resulted from his many speculations and efforts to find new "laws of logic" for biology. His hypothesis on micelles is an example.

Overton, Ernest; 1865-1935

He was born in England and was a distant relative of Charles Darwin. He was seventeen when the family settled in Switzerland because of his mother's chronic illness. He studied there, majoring in botany. After he obtained his doctorate, he worked for two semesters with Strasburger in

Bonn. In 1890, he became a *Dozent* at the University of Zurich. There followed several years as an assistant with the Institute of Physiology in Würzburg. As of 1907, he was Professor of Pharmacology at the University of Lund (Sweden). His research included, the lipid theory of permeability and of narcosis, the physiology of nerves and muscles, and the reduction division in pollen mother cells.

Pasteur, Louis, 1822-1895
Relative to the other biographical notes, it would require pages to adequately describe the accomplishments of this world-famous French chemist and biologist. Let us mention a few landmarks: the foundations of modern bacteriology, the microbic origin of fermentation and vaccination.

Pflüger, Eduard Friedrich Wilhelm; 1829-1910
He was a Professor of Physiology at the University of Bonn. His research covered the physiology of muscles, heat regulation and nutrition. His periodical, *Pflügers Archiv für die gesamte Physiologie* enjoyed an excellent reputation.

Pringsheim, Nathanael; 1824-1894
He studied in Breslau, Leipzig and Berlin. In Berlin, he participated for a time in the revolution of 1848. He was a *Dozent* at the university, but his research was done in a private laboratory. He was a professor at the University of Jena for a time until he returned to Berlin in order to devote himself completely to research. Besides Pfeffer, who worked in Pringsheim's laboratory, there were several other botanists working there who would also become famous. Pringsheim was responsible for the impulse to form the *Deutsche Botanische Gesellschaft* in 1882. In addition, he was the founder of the *Jahrbücher für wissenschaftliche Botanik*, a leading journal oriented toward experimental

research. (After he died, the *Jahrbücher* were edited by Pfeffer, and then by Strasburger). Pringsheim published many papers of value on the development of lower plants.

Purkinje, Johannes Evangelista; 1787-1869

He was of Czech nationality. He studied theology in his native Bohemia, but shortly before being ordained into the priesthood, he turned to philosophy and medicine. His doctor's thesis about the sense of vision is strongly influenced by Goethe's theory of colours. It was thanks to Goethe's personal influence that he was given a professorship at the University of Breslau. Many important research results on the anatomy and physiology of animals and humans originated from his private laboratory in Breslau. A physiological institute at the university was created due to his efforts. After it had been constructed, he turned his interests more to writing. Purkinje is often credited as being the founder of the first physiological institute in Germany. However, it was Carl August Sigmund Schultze (1795-1877) who first founded such an institute in Freiburg in 1821 (Nauck, Freiburg, *Ber. Naturforsch. Ges.*, 40, 147, 1950). Purkinje's last university appointment brought him back to Prague. There, he devoted himself — now as Purkyne — primarily to Czech national concerns.

Rubner, Max; 1854-1932

Professor of Physiology at the universities in Marburg and Berlin. He was the founder of a modern nutrition theory.

Sachs, Julius; 1832-1897

Sachs would have become a seaman and not a botanist if Purkinje had not taken him — an orphan at seventeen — along with his family to Prague. After six years, Sachs left

Purkinje, probably in part because of differing political views. Sachs was an admirer of Bismark; Purkinje was a dedicated Czech patriot. Sachs spent two years in Tharandt as a teaching assistant at the Academy of Horticulture and Forestry. In 1881, he became professor at the Academy of Horticulture in Bonn-Poppelsdorf, and next, at the University of Würzburg. Sachs was one of the most successful teachers in the new field of plant physiology, and he is rightly looked upon as the founder of this field. Many foreign scholars, including Hugo de Vries, came to work with him. Sachs wrote excellent text books (which have been translated into English).

Spemann, Hans; 1869-1941

He was a professor of zoology at the University of Rostock and the University of Freiburg. Between the two appointments, he worked at the *Kaiser Wilhelm Institut für Biologie* in Berlin. In 1935, he was awarded the Nobel Prize for his research in the physiology of the development of amphibian embryos.

Stahl, Ernst; 1848-1919

He was born in Alsace. He studied in Strassburg and then in Halle. After the war of 1870-71, he, as well as De Bary, moved from Holle to Strassburg. There followed a position as *Dozent* at the University of Würzburg under Sachs. He returned to Strassburg as a university professor. His final position was *Ordinarius* at the University of Jena. He worked in various areas of physiology, and especially on questions of ecology. He worked in the wake of Darwin's theory of selectivity, constantly searching for a purpose in every anatomical, morphological or biochemical peculiarity.

Strasburger, Eduard; 1844-1912

He was born in Warsaw. When he was eleven, his family sent him to live in a protestant minister's home in Görlitz where he was to perfect his command of German. The pastor played an important role in stimulating Strasburger's interest in plants. After attending the *Gymnasium* in Warsaw, the eighteen-year-old was sent to Paris to learn a commercial trade and the French language. However, he was more interested in lectures at the Sorbonne, visits to the *Jardin des Plantes*, and botanical excursions. Eventually, Strasburger studied botany in Warsaw, Jena and Bonn. In Bonn, he was most impressed by Julius Sachs. He worked as an assistant for N. Pringsheim in Jena, and he gained his doctorate at the University of Jena. At the age of twenty-three, he passed his examinations for admission to the faculty at the University of Warsaw. His *Habilitation* thesis was submitted in German and in Polish. However, he had no prospects for advancement because of the system in Poland which, in those days, was a part of the Russian Empire. Two years later, he became a professor at the University of Jena. In 1880, he accepted a new appointment in Bonn. He is one of the founders of modern cytology. He investigated the formation and division of cells and recognized the role of the cell nucleus as the carrier of genetic information. He made this finding at about the same time it was made by the zoologist O. Hertwig. The *Lehrbuch der Botanik für Hochschulen* was founded through his initiative. It is still known as the "Strasburger," and up to now, it has had thirty German editions. It has appeared in nearly as many editions in eight foreign languages.

Staudinger, Hermann; 1881-1965

A chemist, whose last position was Professor of Chemistry at the University of Freiburg. In 1953, he was awarded the Nobel Prize for Chemistry in recognition of his pioneering work in macro-molecular chemistry.

Traube, Moritz; 1826-1894

A private scholar. He studied chemistry under Liebig in Giessen and later, he studied medicine. He took over the family wine business, and he installed a private laboratory. His special interest was the study of the oxidation process in organisms.

Van't Hoff, Jacobus Hendricus; 1852-1911

A Dutch Chemist. His investigations covered the asymmetric structure of carbon atoms, the influence of temperature on chemical equilibrium, and the Theory of Solutions. In 1901, he was the first person to receive the Nobel Prize for Chemistry. At the end of his career, he held the position of Research Professor of the Prussian Academy of Sciences and Honorary Professor at Berlin University.

Warburg, Otto Heinrich; 1883-1970

Biochemist and physiologist. In 1931, he was awarded the Nobel Prize for Medicine and Physiology in recognition of his research on respiratory enzymes. He was the author of many papers on the biochemistry of plant and animal cells. Among other subjects he also wrote on photosynthesis. From 1931 until he died, Warburg was the director of the Kaiser-Wilhelm-Institute (now, Max-Planck-Institute) for Cell Physiology in Berlin. Obstinacy helped him to great achievements, but it also led him to maintain a rigid stand once he had taken a position. When he defended his theory on cancer with vehemence, it was evident that he was not willing to make a distinction between cause and symptoms.

Weismann, August; 1834-1914

He began as a medical doctor and later became a zoologist. As a professor at the University of Freiburg, Weismann was an ardent advocate of evolutionary teaching and Darwinism — concepts which were still hotly disputed at the time. He used reasoning and experiments to fight Lamarck's teachings stating that acquired characteristics could be inherited. In teaching about the continuity of the "germplasm" Weismann was on the right path in searching for what is now called genetic information (largely stored in the chromosomes). "The centre point of my concept is that the transfer of the principle of selectivity exists at all levels in living units . . . it will endure, even if everything around it should prove to be perishable." (Quoted from the foreword to *Vorträge über Deszendenztheorie*, 1902.)

INDEX OF NAMES

Names which appear in the main text in Notes and in Biographical Notes are listed. Other names appear in Publications by Collaborators and in Visiting Scholars.

The underlined numbers refer to names in the Biographical Notes.

INDEX OF SUBJECTS AND PLACES